Peasants in Revolt

Latin American Monographs, No. 28
Institute of Latin American Studies
The University of Texas at Austin

PEASANTS IN REVOLT

A Chilean Case Study, 1965-1971

James Petras and Hugo Zemelman Merino

Translated by Thomas Flory

PUBLISHED FOR THE INSTITUTE OF LATIN AMERICAN
STUDIES BY THE UNIVERSITY OF TEXAS PRESS,
AUSTIN AND LONDON

Library of Congress Cataloging in Publication Data

Petras, James F   1937-
    Peasants in revolt.

    (Latin American monographs, no. 28)
    Translated from the author's unpublished ms.
    1. Peasantry—Chile—Case studies. 2. Peasant
uprising—Chile—Case studies. 3. Political
participation—Chile—Case studies. I. Zemelman
Merino, Hugo, 1931-   joint author. II. Title.
III. Series: Latin American monographs (Austin, Tex.)
no. 28.
HD506.P4813   322.4'2'0983   72-1578
ISBN 0-292-76404-9

309.183
P49p

Manufactured in the United States of America

Dedicated to the memory of

MAURICE LEFEVBRE

friend, scholar, and fighter

CONTENTS

PREFACE

This study analyzes one instance of illegal and violent peasant political action in Chile: the seizure of a largely abandoned private landed estate. In the course of interviews and discussions with peasant leaders and followers we were impressed by the degree of rational thought and calculation that preceded the illegal land seizure. The standard image of peasants as passive, ignorant, submissive—in other words, traditional subjects—was not found. Nor did we see peasants lending themselves as the docile tools of urban agitators or "extremists." The emergence of an alert and active peasantry is probably the result of the emergence of a more tolerant political ambience (the absence of violent repression), of successful organizing efforts, and in part at least of the peasants' own struggles. Our case illustrates some of the rational components of revolutionary mass action and some of the democratic possibilities that might be realized.

The land seizure under study occurred during the first year of the Eduardo Frei government. This government promised to provide land for 100,000 peasant proprietors in six years and ended up with a little over 20,000 new landholders. Nevertheless, strong social pressures were generated by the growth of a broad peasant movement, which embraced approximately one-third of all the economically active landless peasantry. Union organization, strikes, and occasional land seizures improved the socioeconomic position of the peasants. The positive results of radical political action from below contrasted sharply with the generally dismal picture that emerged from Chile's experiment with the Christian Democratic version of evolutionary politics.

While land seizures were infrequent at the time when the farm under study was occupied (1965), the farm's seizure served as a reference point in subsequent political and social conflicts in the area. More important, the peasant movement in Chile went through a series of phases that can be briefly summarized as follows:

1. Massive peasant unionization oriented toward collective bargaining rights, minimum wage payments, and salary increases;
2. Continuation of unionization and bread-and-butter demands, but with increasing use of strikes to pressure for land reform;
3. Organization of national unions and arrangement of collective bargaining agreements on a provincial level, leading first to province-wide strikes (as opposed to strikes on individual farms) and finally to a nation-wide strike (May 1970) demanding the acceleration of the agrarian reform.

Thus, by the end of the Frei period, the countryside as a whole was organized, politicized, and prepared for a massive and rapid land reform.

During the period between the election of Salvador Allende in September 1970 and November when he took office, scores of farms were occupied. By the end of January 1971, three months after Chile's first Socialist president had taken office, over three hundred farms had been occupied by the peasant movement. Unlike the Frei administration, the Allende government decided to accelerate the land-expropriation process—taking over twelve hundred farms during the first eight months in office (compared with fifteen hundred farms during the six years of the Frei government). Under the Socialist government these land seizures served as an important catalytic agent hastening the legal process, while under the previous government land seizures had been much more of a substitute for weak executive leadership.

The original dynamism and radicalism that appeared in the initial stages of the land occupation, however, were largely transitory. As our study of Culiprán suggests, peasant radicalism is at best an ambiguous phenomenon—expressing both a profound desire to obtain land, including the willingness to use violent means, and a strong sense of property ownership once in a position to exploit the land. The end result of the land invasion in our case study illustrates this process of bourgeoisification: the once insurgent peasants turned entrepreneurs exploiting labor and accumulating property and capital at the expense of their former *compañeros.* Given the agricultural goals of the Christian Democratic government and the national political, economic, and cultural context in which the land transfer took place, it was almost inevitable that the peasants in Culiprán would develop a business farmer's mentality. What is not established by our study and what remains to be studied in the future is whether the land-reform beneficiaries under Allende's Socialist government can be oriented toward collective ownership or whether the orientation to private entrepreneurship that we have observed in Culiprán will be repeated in the new political context.

The farm Culiprán, which we studied, is located in the municipality of Melipilla, Santiago province in the fertile Central Valley of Chile. It lies less than two hours from the capital. In October 1965 after a series of encounters with the landowner and fruitless attempts to have their problems solved by public officials, peasants seized control of the farm, armed themselves, and prepared to resist forcible removal. Under considerable pressure the Christian Democratic Frei government expropriated the farm and established a land colony (*asentamiento*), within which the peasants worked collectively for three years. At the end of this period the peasants would vote for either individual owners, collective ownership, or a combination of the two. As the Epilogue suggests, the peasants voted for a combination of individual and collective ownership, but with a clear emphasis on the former.

The illegal violent action by the peasants and its effects on their behavior and political and social attitudes is the subject of this work. Data were collected in January-June 1966 through taped in-depth interviews with twelve peasants: four leaders, six followers, and two peasants who opposed the action. We have utilized the semistructured interview and six months of participatory observation. The interview was developed from an ideal typology of peasant consciousness that has been useful in the ordering of information. This information was collected directly from the peasants themselves and can be found in the Appendix of this monograph. Care has been taken to see that a faithful transcription of the informants' language has been presented. Not all the material collected has been used in the analysis itself, because it did not seem necessary, given the exploratory nature of the investigation. Instead, we have selected those interviews that seemed to express with most clarity and coherence the different attitudes toward the takeover.

We would like to thank Professor Marion Brown for his suggestions, comments, and criticisms and Professor Thomas Flory for his editorial suggestions and translation.

Peasants in Revolt

1. Introduction

To fully understand the data collected in our study of the *fundo* Culiprán, it is necessary to consider the historical context to which it is linked. The development of peasant political consciousness is not a process that takes place overnight; nor is it simply the result of external factors. The development and the expression of political ideas, as well as of opinions on national and local issues, are products of present conditions. But they are no less the results of a historical process in which certain attitudes and actions have been chosen rather than others.

As will be seen, certain key individuals act as the bearers of traditions and earlier attitudes that respond to the stimulus of new possibilities and experiences to facilitate the expression of desires previously repressed.

The first part of this book deals with two interrelated factors: social conditions and political behavior. The social and economic conditions that mark the area under study provide an image of the character and dynamics of the development process. On the other hand, comparisons of rural and urban life at the county and provincial levels point out the tensions created by the process of uneven development of services and social benefits. Data are presented regarding that behavior which produces political changes, and this behavior is examined by comparing electoral tendencies at the regional and national levels. It is hoped that both the direction and the rate of development of political attitudes on the *fundo* Culiprán will throw some light on the process as a whole.

We recognize the limitations imposed by the use of electoral behavior as an indicator of political attitudes, for voting can only be used as a very imperfect approximation of certain general political tendencies. In spite of these limitations, however, the existence of certain patterns can be shown; and it is in this barometric sense—not as a definitive expression of the popular will—that we consider electoral conduct applicable.

One last consideration may be relevant. Some may object that it is incongruous to suppose that the illegal and violent occupation of private property by a collective movement is in intimate relation with the development of civic responsibility. This study is an attempt not to diagnose the emergence of citizenship in the juridical sense, but rather to describe it as it emerges in reality—as the free and independent expression of political rights. There is no novelty in considering the political situation and the economic base as necessary to the development of this form of citizenship. The idea is as old as Aristotle.

The Social Context of Culiprán

The *comuna* of Melipilla includes both the town of that name and the great *fundos* that surround it. According to the census of 1960, its population was 40,890 persons, 58.5 percent of whom were considered "rural" (*campesina*). Agriculture is the most important activity, and 54.5 percent of the active population is engaged in it. Only 8.9 percent of the population is occupied in the manufacturing industries. There is, however, a sizable service sector (33.5%), which primarily serves the surrounding area.

Unlike that of other rural areas, especially those adjacent to large cities, the population of Melipilla is not declining. Between 1952 and 1960 the average annual rate of demographic growth was 2.1 percent. Emigration appears to be mainly by the female population, for 54.8 percent of Melipilla's rural population is male—though they represent only 47.5 percent of the town of Melipilla, and only 46.3 percent of urban Santiago. This emigration is largely attributable to the relative lack of economic opportunities for women in the countryside, which traditionally requires the labor of men. In Melipilla only 13.7 percent of all women are employed in nonagricultural sectors, while the average for the nation is 20 percent and rises to 27.9 percent in the province of Santiago. The lack of opportunities in rural areas and the greater possibilities of work in urban areas influence the female peasants more than the males.

The social and educational conditions of the *comuna* of Melipilla seem to be decidedly inferior to those of the province as a whole or even to the national average.

As may be seen in Table 1, Melipilla falls below the provincial and national averages in all categories that measure social development. This

TABLE 1

Social, Medical, and Educational Conditions
(The *comuna* of Melipilla, the province of Santiago,
and the national average)

Condition	Melipilla	Santiago	National Average
Houses with:			
Potable water	40.8%	78.4%	53.0%
Electric light	64.4%	87.5%	64.5%
Indoor plumbing	25.1%	64.3%	40.9%
Death certificates			
registered by a physician	63.0%	94.9%	72.1%
Literacy			
Men	76.6%	92.0%	84.8%
Women	76.8%	90.0%	82.4%

Source: Armand Mattelart, *Atlas Social de las comunas de Chile* (Santiago: Editorial del Pacifico, 1965), pp. 46, 48.

fact points out the inequality that characterizes the Chilian social situation; for, even if the province of Santiago is taken as an exceptional case, it is only in the category of electric light that Melipilla approaches the national average.

A further breakdown of rural and urban conditions in Melipilla (Table 2) reveals a social duality: conditions in urban Melipilla are much closer to urban conditions at the provincial and national levels than are those of rural Melipilla. In each category the conditions of rural Melipilla not only are considerably inferior to the national and provincial averages, but also are decidedly worse than those of the town of Melipilla.

These social statistics (and to a lesser extent those regarding education) clearly show the differences between town and country. The characteristic imbalance in social development indicates, then, that urban development has been carried out in large part at the expense of the rural sectors. At this point it may be deduced that the urban progress of Chile has been

TABLE 2

Social and Educational Conditions in Rural and
Urban Melipilla

Condition	Rural	Urban
Houses with:		
Potable water	11.3%	75.6%
Electric light	45.8%	86.2%
Indoor plumbing	14.7%	37.3%
Literacy		
Men	66.6%	87.4%
Women	68.2%	83.8%
Average number of inhabitants per dwelling	7	5.5

Source: Mattelart, *Atlas Social,* pp. 46, 48.

built on the sacrifices of the rural population—thus creating an evident
social duality. In practice, the general process of development and its
concomitant irregularities are both aspects of the same reality.

Social services in rural Melipilla are far from the national urban standards. However, social conditions in the rural sector of the municipality
are considerably superior to the national rural average—though they fall
short of the provincial rural level (Table 3). These minimum figures for
Melipilla are very low; but, excepting literacy, they are somewhat higher
than the national rural average, which has not even reached these minimal
levels. Perhaps it is in this type of *comuna*, where some development has
just begun to take place, that rural tensions become particularly acute.

Social conditions in rural Melipilla are linked to an economic system
dominated by large landholders. Whereas 2,640 landholdings in the area
occupy only 864.4 hectares of the total, there are 32 estates that occupy
at least 82,500 hectares (Table 4). Though the *minifundios* are twelve
times more numerous than all other landholdings, the greatest concentration of land continues to be in the hands of the *latifundistas*. Eighty-five
percent of these large holdings are the property of individuals; the rest
belong to companies and other institutions. Together, the sharecroppers,
empleados, and *inquilinos* (tenant workers) of Melipilla possess some 3.5
percent of all the local land, or almost 4,000 hectares. The active agricul-

TABLE 3

Social and Educational Conditions
(The *comuna* of Melipilla, rural provincial Santiago,
and the national rural average)

Condition	Melipilla	Santiago	National Average
Houses with:			
Potable water	11.3%	17.6%	3.8%
Electric light	45.8%	53.0%	19.4%
Indoor plumbing	14.7%	18.3%	7.6%
Literacy:			
Men	66.6%	70.6%	68.8%
Women	68.2%	72.5%	63.5%
Average number of inhabitants per dwelling	7	6.3	5

Source: Mattelart, *Atlas Social*, pp. 46, 48.

TABLE 4

Number of Landowners by Size of Holding
and Percentage of Total Area

Size of Holding	Number	% of Total Area
Less than one hectare	2,640	0.8
Small (1-99.9 hectares)	139	2.4
Medium (100-999.9 hectares)	48	8.0
Large (1,000 hectares and more)	32	88.8

Source: Servicio Nacional de Estadística y Censos, *Censo Nacional Agrícola y Ganadera* (Santiago: República de Chile, 1955), vol. 5.

tural labor force of Melipilla totals 5,086 persons and may be subdivided as shown in Table 5.

The level of agricultural mechanization in Melipilla is relatively high in comparison with that of the other *comunas* in the province. There is an average of more than one tractor per estate, and Melipilla has been quick to accept most new developments in agricultural machinery.

Political Participation in Melipilla

The oldest available election records indicate that around 1925 Melipilla had a nucleus of leftist opposition. In that year the candidate of the left

TABLE 5

Divisions of Agricultural Labor Force
in Melipilla

Type	Number	%
Owners who work their own land	255	5.2
Administrators, technicians, foremen	443	8.9
Tenants, skilled laborers, sharecroppers	2,030	39.9
Common laborers	2,347	46.0
	5,075	100.0

Source: *Censo Nacional Agrícola Ganadero.*

coalition, José Santos Salas, polled 13.7 percent of the Melipilla vote in his campaign against the candidate of the traditional right, Emiliano Figueroa Larraín. This figure becomes all the more significant when it is remembered that the candidacy of Salas was announced in Santiago only shortly before the election, so that there was scarcely time for his name to become known in the countryside. In spite of the lack of publicity, the campaign of the populist left had considerable national impact, and the birth of "populist leftism" in Melipilla was surpassed in Santiago province, where Salas acquired 39 percent of the vote. That Melipilla's support for populism did not reach the provincial average reveals the great influence the traditional groups still wielded in the countryside.

In the next election (1931), the two Communist candidates, Elías Lafferte (Stalinist) and Manuel Hidalgo (Trotskyist), together obtained less than 1 percent of the total vote. The strength of rural populism was manifest in the 1932 elections when Marmaduque Grove, the Socialist candidate, cornered 16.1 percent of the vote. Grove's showing takes on considerably greater importance when it is remembered that he not only was opposed by the traditional right, but that he also faced Arturo Alessandri and the moderately reformist Radical party as well. Nevertheless, it should be noted once again that the Grove vote was considerably higher in Santiago province (33%) than in Melipilla (16.1%), while declining slightly in relation to Salas's vote of 1925 in the province (39%).

Although Salas and, especially, Grove proposed an agrarian reform (which may be used as a barometer of rural populist leftism), the presidential candidates of 1938, 1942, and 1949 can scarcely be said to have offered any clear alternative to the status quo. The Radical party never seriously tried to elaborate an agrarian reform, and during the Popular

Front years (the term of Aguirre Cerda) the development of a rural movement to promote agrarian reform was frustrated, and even the unionization of peasants was put off.

Faced with the agrarian question, the middle-class Radical party presidents proved little different from their traditional right-wing adversaries. It was only in 1952 and in the following elections of 1958 and 1964 that political forces arose that, however vaguely, can be identified with a policy of agrarian reform. Taking 1952 as a base year, three political tendencies were clearly defined: (1) the decay of the traditional right; (2) the rapid increase in supporters of the left; and (3) the cyclical pattern of development of populist movements.

The most marked of these trends is the demise of the traditional right. In 1952, the candidates of the right—Pedro Enrique Alfonso and Arturo Matte Larraín—received 60.2 percent of the total vote in the *comuna* of Melipilla; in 1958 Alessandri and Luis Bossay collected 48.9 percent; and in 1964 Julio Durán polled only 2.1 percent of the Melipilla vote. Between 1952 and 1964, the traditional right lost more than 90 percent of its voters in the *comuna*. On the other hand, the Chilean left enjoyed an increase in strength that partially matched the downward trend of the right. In 1952, Allende attracted 1.4 percent of the votes in Melipilla; but in 1958 his vote rose to 25.1 percent, and in 1964 to 34 percent.

The rising and falling fortunes of the Ibañista populist movement represent the third important political trend, though the Ibañista movement has been in large part replaced by the advent of the Christian Democrats, who combine the characteristics of both populism and corporativism. In 1952, 38.5 percent of Melipilla's votes went to Carlos Ibáñez del Campo. The failure of Ibañismo brought a temporary regression of corporative populism, and many voters turned to the left. In 1958 Frei polled only 22.1 percent.

While there are important differences between the Ibáñez presidential victory of 1952 and that of Frei in 1964, there are also important similarities in the nature of the political campaigns. Both Ibáñez and Frei engaged in populist-style appeals and attracted a large number of lower-class rural voters who previously had followed the lead of conservative landowners; both candidates rejected the traditional right and the Marxist left; both candidates seemed to articulate a populist political style—they rejected liberal individualism as well as socialist collectivism and attempted to formulate a "third way," which focused on forging social bonds across class lines.

Unlike Ibáñez, supported by an amorphous *ad hoc* coalition, Frei was the candidate of a well-organized political party. Nevertheless, the Frei campaign, like Ibáñez's, was largely dominated by the personality of the candidate: the image that was projected was of a strong paternal figure interested in the problems of the poor. Both Ibáñez and Frei were supported by a heterogeneous polyclass coalition, a coalition that was built on the basis of an ideology that rejected the politics of class struggle and spoke of regenerating society (Ibáñez) or creating a new "communitarian society" (Frei). Both favored the incorporation of the excluded masses into society without the total displacement of the elites. Hence, both in political style and to a substantial degree in political appeal, Frei and Ibáñez can be placed in a common political tradition despite their other differences.

In 1964, Frei's populist campaign and agrarian reform orientation won him 63.4 percent of the Melipilla *comuna*. A disproportionate percentage of this vote was contributed by sectors that earlier had been those most clearly identified with traditional agrarian conservatism. The breakdown by sexes of the Melipilla vote shows this tendency very plainly (Table 6).

TABLE 6

A Comparison of Presidential Voting Patterns,
1958-1964

Candidate	Year	Men (%)	Women (%)
Allende	1958	28.4	19.2
Allende	1964	39.1	28.7
Alessandri-Bossay	1958	47.5	51.9
Durán	1964	2.4	1.9
Frei	1958	20.4	15.2
Frei	1964	58.6	69.4

Source: Registro Electoral, Santiago.

Among the Melipillan men, Allende's vote increased 10.7 percent from 1958 to 1964, but his increase among the women was only 9.5 percent. In the case of Frei, however, the rise was 38.2 percent among male peasants and 44.2 percent among the females. As the rural vote turned away from its traditional conservative stance, it generally tended toward the populism of Frei; but what is more important within this general scheme is that nearly four out of every ten male rural voters gave their support to the Socialist candidate—a surprising and an abrupt change of attitude since the early 1950's, when little more than 1 percent voted Socialist. If 1952 is taken as a base year for the comparison of the growth of leftist and populist political trends, it is evident that the more radical tendencies are growing almost twice as rapidly as the corporativist formula, despite the fact that among rural females populism seems to be growing slightly more rapidly than the more radical alternatives (Table 7).

TABLE 7

A Comparison of Socialist and Populist Voting Trends,
1952 and 1964

Candidate	1952		1964		Percentage Growth	
	Men	Women (%)	Men	Women (%)	Men	Women
Allende (Socialist)	1.6	0.9	39.1	28.7	37.5	27.8
Ibáñez & Frei (Populist)	40.2	34.8	58.6	69.4	18.4	34.6

Source: Registro Electoral, Santiago.

As shown in Table 8, the growth of radicalism is most pronounced between 1952 and 1958, settling into a rather slower pace from 1958 until 1964. The period of the left's greatest growth coincides with the period of decline in populism during the Ibáñez years. This would seem to indicate an important number of ex-Ibáñistas' turning to the left. Similarly, a sudden decline of the traditional right took place between 1958 and 1964—the period in which popular corporativism shows its greatest

TABLE 8

A Comparison of Populist and Socialist Voting Trends
in 1952 and 1958 Presidential Elections

Year	Left (%)	Populism (%)
1952	1.4	38.5
1958	25.1	22.1

Source: Registro Electoral, Santiago.

increase (Table 9). Apparently, then, a great number of the voters of the traditional right found their way into the camp of popular corporativism at the time. Such political changes, especially those tending toward the left, are occurring much more swiftly in rural Melipilla than in the province as a whole (Table 10).

TABLE 9

A Comparison of Populist and Traditional Rightist
Voting Trends in Presidential Elections,
1958 and 1964

Year	Left (%)	Populism (%)	Traditional Right (%)
1958	25.1	22.1	48.9
1964	34.0	63.4	2.1

Source: Registro Electoral, Santiago.

TABLE 10

A Comparison of Presidential Voting Trends in the
Municipality of Melipilla and the
Province of Santiago

Year	Melipilla (*comuna*) (%)	Province of Santiago (%)	% Growth of Left Melipilla	Santiago
1952	1.4	7.1	32.6	28.8
1964	34.0	35.9		

Source: Registro Electoral, Santiago.

On a more general level, the irregularity in the growth of political radicalism (its more rapid growth in the rural areas) may be the direct result of irregularities in social and economic development. The desire to reach the standard of living of neighboring cities and towns may give birth to political radicalism as part of the effort toward obtaining these objectives.

But here a warning is in order: during the elections of 1964 the alternatives offered to the electorate in party programs were very similar, and it is possible that differing electoral attitudes were largely a reflection of the campaign itself. The campaigns of both candidates attached great importance to a "profound agrarian reform." This fact, as may be seen in the interviews, had a significant effect on the postelection period that concerns us.

One final consideration is very important in the political evolution of the countryside. Electoral reforms put into effect at the end of the forties, in 1958, and again in 1962, extended the franchise to women, practically eliminated the possibility of buying or manipulating votes by introducing the single ballot (*voto único*), and made voter registration almost obligatory by attaching important social benefits to it.

The electoral laws broadening suffrage were accompanied by other changes in society and, especially, within political parties (Table 11). The sudden introduction into the system of massive numbers of rural female voters—generally less politicized and more indirectly involved in production than the males—greatly strengthened the base of the traditional right and, later, that of the Christian Democrats (Table 12). In fact, women represented 62 percent of the Melipillanos voting for the first time in 1964, justifying the assumption that a solid majority of all first-time voters cast their ballots for Frei in 1964.

TABLE 11

Total Vote in the Presidential Elections of 1952, 1958, and 1964

Year	Melipilla (*comuna*)	National	% Increase (Melipilla)	% Increase (national)
1952	4,667	945,131	*1952-1958*	*1952-1958*
1958	5,655	1,235,552	21.1	29.5
1964	11,692	2,512,157	*1958-1964*	*1958-1964*
			106.8	103.3

Source: Registro Electoral, Santiago.

TABLE 12

New Voters in Melipilla: Percentage of Votes
for Traditional Right and Christian
Democratic Party

Year	Traditional Right*		Christian Democrats	
	Men	Women	Men	Women
1952	58.2	64.2	–	–
1958	47.5	51.9	20.4	25.2
1964	2.4	1.9	58.6	69.4

*Alfonso and Matte Larraín in 1952; Alessandri and Bossay in 1958; Durán in 1964.
Source: Registro Electoral, Santiago.

2. Political Change: The Formation of a New Structure of Authority

The process of change at Culiprán was cumulative and complex. Long-established norms were challenged indirectly and through devious means. Protest was repressed: the protestors were deprived of their livelihood and expelled from the community. New movements began and old leaders went into other activities or were co-opted. The old structure continued, bearing within it members whose memories of older struggles continued dormant. Discontent became latent, awaiting propitious moments to express itself. Yet minor changes in the structure of agriculture accumulated over time, and isolation lessened; external political agencies looking for means of gaining power fanned the desire for land and justice; a new literate generation of young peasants emerged, nourished on the ideas of equality and not yet having experienced the defeats and humiliations of their fathers. These periods of slow change were characterized by informal discussions and interchange of ideas—stories told by relatives, friends, or those on the farm who visited outside were related and passed on by word of mouth.

Traditional relations based on deference and obedience had been subject to popular resistance in the past, though repression and sanctions usually limited resistance to desperate moments or times when external forces appeared capable of neutralizing the weight of official violence. Interviewee Five recalled the peasant mobilization of an earlier period. He described the emerging resistance, the subsequent defeat, and the recent resurgence:

> Politics came to a stop here many years ago during the time of Pedro Aguirre Cerda. There was a revolution on the *fundo* and they let us stay provided we didn't get involved in politics again. At that time—in 1940 and 1941—the Socialist party was organized here, and since then the *compañeros* have kept the idea—the fighting idea—of taking advantage of the right time to seize the land. We always have had the intention of finding a better life—of living a little easier. Pedro Aguirre Cerda was the presidential candidate of the Socialist party. How many of us were there? Some 150 or less. The whole *fundo* was involved—it was the "product" of the Socialists. When the party was organized we began to go out to Santiago, San Antonio, and Noviciado to make propaganda for Don Pedro. We went to several places. I was head of the militia because all the Socialist parties had militias. It was a separate group that had to keep order in case there was some trouble.
>
> In Melipilla they were afraid to make propaganda because there were many rightists, so the peasant *compañeros* came to us. Isn't that funny? That's right, in Melipilla they were so few they didn't count for anything, but here on the *fundo* we got three truckloads of men together. When we got to Melipilla they had everything for us from rubber stamps to those clubs the cops use. We divided up: one stood guard, others painted slogans, and others put up posters. They came to find us one night because all the rightist propaganda was ready and they were afraid to put up the propaganda of Don Pedro. At dawn we were in the town. It was just getting light when we left, and the whole town, the plaza, and all the major streets were covered with slogans and propaganda.
>
> It was then that the Socialist party was organized here on the *fundo*, and three *compañeros* were kicked out. The *patrón* booted them out because they didn't want to get out of the party. The *patrón* gave them that advice and offered them 1,001 things to get them to leave the party but they wouldn't, so he came and threw them out. And my father-in-law was one of those who got the axe. I was living with him, and I arrived at just the right time—when they were moving his things out—and said to the administrator: "Señor, I wasn't told anything. Ask them not to throw my things in the street." Then he told me that he'd taken my things out because he was kicking me out, too. So I looked for another place. I went to a compadre's place and stayed with him. That very afternoon I came back and moved my stuff over there and I stayed with my compadre for a year. Yes, the *patrón*

threw them out; he fired two here, and he fired others in Bajo. They just had to leave, that's all, because he kicked them all out.[1]

What happened then? What's happened up to now? Well, there was the change of presidents, and we began to take heart when Señor Eduardo Frei was elected. We said, "Now Señor Frei has to help, he has to help us." In those days the leaders of the Socialist party didn't come around anymore. The only ones who came were from the Christian Democrats and the Communist party. And they also came around to campaign for the election of deputies and senators. So we were encouraged again and we said, "Now we have to organize ourselves again."

The tradition and history of deference were thus accompanied by a certain popular resistance: inarticulate and inchoate attempts by peasants to "better their lot." The countryside appeared in many ways as it had a century before, yet it was possible to discover among individual peasants the mode by which traditional relationships were imposed and retained. The periodic use of selective violence and the everyday absolute control over conduct in social relations are variables that have only infrequently been considered in discovering the sources of established authority in the countryside. Socialization of the peasantry into a repressive society that is paternalistic and authoritarian was the *outcome* of a system of authority that more frequently than not possessed the means to enforce its will through violence—with or without the approval of constitutions and laws. Usually, in fact, the state itself assumed the duty and obligation of enforcing the authority of the owner. In some cases the owner himself was the lawmaker.

The peasants did not passively accept the "law of the lord," but formed their own ideas of right and wrong, of what they received and what they *should* receive in exchange for their labor. The earlier "moral economy," the semireligious idea that each man should earn enough to maintain his family, still was held against the "modern" idea of individual profit maximization. Traditional relations were viewed, at a minimum, as means to secure a livelihood. Alongside this traditional attitude there also sprang up

[1] The peasants appear unaware that one of the key reasons for the repression and containment of peasant insurgency in the late 1930's and early 1940's was the acceptance by the Socialist and Communist parties of ministerial and parliamentary responsibility for a Radical government committed to the status quo in the countryside. The political leaders referred to in the quote are Pedro Aguirre Cerda, a member of the Radical party supported by the Popular Front coalition that included the Socialist and Communist parties, whose term of office was from 1938 until 1941, when he died; and Eduardo Frei, a leader in the Christian Democratic party, who was elected president in 1964 for a six-year period.

from time to time the desire to work for oneself rather than be exploited by the owner. This latent desire turned the peasant's eyes toward the land that he worked for someone else.

Because the obligations and responsibilities between peasant and owner were intricately interconnected, rapid changes in one area were likely to set in motion a whole series of other changes. The final result could mean basic shifts in values and perception of status and, in some cases, revolutionary activity. The disintegration of the traditional structure of authority in Culiprán was thus neither a cataclysmic action nor the result of purely autonomous impersonal social and economic factors.[2]

Uneven Development and Social Change

The process of modernization has been uneven in Chile, largely by-passing rural society, but in recent years deep inroads have been made in certain areas previously influenced by traditional modes of behavior. Agriculture has been commercialized and oriented toward the market; owners are oriented toward maximizing profits. Traditional social relations served as a convenient mode of controlling the labor force and preventing disruption of the productive process. The landowners frequently calculated their production and marketed their goods in accordance with market prices while usually maintaining payments in kind and other devices of the earlier "natural economy." Within the farm, traditional deference patterns and paternalism persisted; externally the owner sought to maximize his gains as any modern capitalist.

The owner was able to maintain traditional social relations and his modern commercial activity by isolating his labor force from the outside world—preventing the peasants from experiencing the external world. External contacts led the peasants to make comparisons that reflected unfavorably on their social situation.

---

[2] This study focuses on relations between human beings, the patterns of social control and deference and the process by which individuals undertook to change their situation. Impersonal processes do play a significant role in facilitating changes in the structure of authority. What we mean to point up, however, is that these "processes" must be analyzed in terms of how they affect, how they filter through, human beings. The agency of change is living individuals; the activity of individuals is oriented and informed by their awareness of their particular situation and the larger environment that surrounds them. Human consciousness, more specifically political consciousness, itself becomes an important variable affecting the process of change. We will begin by identifying the overall changes taking place in the countryside and then attempt to describe some of the relevant political factors that contribute toward political change.

For a long time the owners were successful in maintaining their authority, largely because of support from official governmental agencies and policies. In recent years, however, modernity has been introduced through several combined processes, all of them tending to undermine the traditional pattern of authority and parallel social relations. These processes are (1) increased communication among peasants and between peasants and the sources promoting agrarian reform, (2) growth of corporate ownership in agriculture, (3) mechanization of production and specialization of labor, (4) cash payments replacing payments in kind, (5) rural-urban migration, and (6) commercialization of agriculture.

The introduction in 1958 of a new voting system, pushed through parliament by an alliance of the center and the left, made it easier for the *inquilinos* and other peasants to vote for the party of their choice, while the emergence of the Christian Democratic movement as a major political force brought issues to their attention that were not legitimate subjects of public discussion and debate in the recent past. These factors in turn facilitated Socialist and Communist political access to the *inquilinos* and the peasantry in general. The large *fundos* became increasingly devoted to production for the market, and new economic forms of agricultural enterprise began to change the face of the countryside. Agricultural corporations gained in importance relative to the large individual landowner, and these corporations now own a significant proportion of the arable land, especially that held in large *fundos*.[3]

A great many of the children of *inquilinos*, as well as of other peasants, have left the countryside for the cities to find work in industry and construction. Through contact with their friends and relatives still in the countryside, these migrants have described experiences that soon become part of the cumulative pressures for change in the peasants' ideas.[4]

[3] For instance, a still incomplete study by Maurice Zeitlin of economic concentration shows that of the twenty largest *fundos* (measured in hectares of first-class land) in the ten agricultural provinces from Aconcagua to Nuble, six, with 29 percent of the land held by the top twenty, belong to corporations; another two, with 9 percent of the land, belong to limited partnerships by inheritance (*comunidades*); two more, with 10 percent of the land, belong to government institutions; the Catholic church has one with 4 percent of the land; and nine individuals own the remaining nine *fundos*, with 49 percent of the land held by these top twenty *fundos*.

[4] The trend toward urbanization in Chile is marked. The 1940 census was the first to note a greater urban than rural population; in 1940, the urban population was estimated at 52.5 percent; in 1952, at 60.2 percent; and in 1960, at 68.9 percent, according to the population censuses of those years. This population growth, however, "has not been accompanied by a proportional increment in industrialization" (CORFO, *Geografía Económica de Chile* [Santiago, Chile: Editorial Universitaria, 1965], pp. 376 ff.). Merwin Bohan and Morton Pomeranz (*Investment in Chile: Basic*

Social Change, Political Development, and Authority

We will here focus on several aspects of the Culiprán situation that will allow a better understanding of the nature of political life in a rural setting. One aspect concerns the pattern of decision-making and the mode by which problems are resolved. Another is the process by which traditional political authority is displaced; another, the forms of authority that can replace it. Such an investigation raises a number of key questions. Is grass roots political activity among peasants possible, and what circumstances activate peasant activists? Is popular rule possible? What are the experiences that produce citizens with a high level of interest and participation, and a sense of political efficacy, confidence, and optimism about the future? Are peasants merely passive instruments of manipulative external elites or are they capable under certain circumstances of manipulating politicians to serve their own ends? How effective are negotiation and bargaining in producing change, and in what circumstances are mass mobilization, illegal activity, and the willingness to practice violence prerequisites for producing necessary changes? What is the relationship between civility and revolution—is the latter a prerequisite for the former? Is a civic culture a postrevolutionary phenomenon?

Political development in Culiprán was a process in which representative organizations and peasant leaders emerged who articulated the interests of previously undifferentiated social forces. Political *experience* was important

---

Information for United States Businessmen [Washington, D.C.: U.S. Government Printing Office, 1960], p. 40) comment: "The growth of cities in every section of the country gives evidence that the rural worker and his family are no longer satisfied to remain in an environment that gives little hope for advancement or improvement."

Our own investigation indicates an *absolute* drop in the number of landless workers (*inquilinos* and wage laborers) between 1935 and 1955. Taking the raw census figures presented for provinces, and summing them, we arrive at the following:

All Provinces			Provinces: Aconcagua-Nuble		
Inquilinos	Wage Laborers	Total	*Inquilinos*	Wage Laborers	Total
1935					
107,906	201,418	309,324	58,701	119,914	178,615
1955					
82,367	176,612	258,979	48,986	101,492	150,478

These figures, to the extent that comparison between them is valid, indicate the vast migration of the rural workers to the city. Thus the indirect contacts that the rural workers who remain are having with the life of the city and of a politicized working class are obviously extensive.

in shaping responses of emerging citizens; this fact suggests that continuity of historical grievances and the presence of older members of previous struggles were important agencies of change. Alongside these traditional historical factors that facilitated change was a new factor: younger members of the community whose frame of reference and alternatives were derived from outside the farm through contacts with the modern world. The interaction of the traditions and experiences carried by the few older peasants and the modern values and sources of legitimacy expressed in the younger groups produced the dynamic fusion that led to conflict with the traditional mechanisms of social control.

Conflict and development must be seen in relational terms; the growth of class consciousness was the outcome of interclass relationships. In Culiprán, political awareness among the peasantry developed in direct response to the negative policies adopted by the traditional authority figures toward the peasants' demands. Rigidity and inflexibility of traditional authority in the face of new demands were important determinants of the direction and development of political consciousness among peasants. Unresponsiveness and ineffectiveness of official governmental channels in mediating demands and solving immediate problems became determinants of peasant political radicalism. The relationship of peasants to urban-based political groups contributed to the development of peasant political skills—the formulating, articulating, and publicizing of issues and problems.

Traditional Authority and Class Struggle

The structure of authority of the *fundo* exhibited many of the characteristics of quasi-absolutist rulership: the decisions were made by the owner, or by administrators whose decision-making power was delegated by the owner, to whom they were solely responsible. Interviewee One recalls that, "before the takeover, the administrator, Don Ligualdo, took care of the problems that came up. We met with him every month, and, if there was trouble with an *inquilino* or something, he decided the problem; and it there was a crime involved it went before the judge. But the administrator was in charge of fixing these things with us individually. If it was a problem where money was needed, he would go to the *patrón* and see about getting that."

Nevertheless, the history of quasi-absolute rule was punctuated by social conflict. In the case of Culiprán, peasant informants revealed that intense social strife and political mobilization occurred in 1920, in 1935-1940, and again in 1946-1947, prior to the current upsurge (1962 to the present). Interviewee One recalled: "I was ten when Arturo Alessandri Palma was elected [1920], and this hacienda was the first to go out on the strike called by the Federación Obrera de Chile [Chilean Workers' Federation]. After that we marched to Melipilla." He pointed to the gains achieved through struggle: "In those days my father was making 80 cobres as an *inquilino* on the hacienda, but after the strike he made 1.20 pesos— they gave him a raise of 40 cobres."

Contact with the outside through military conscription and the political experience of registering to vote may have prepared some of the Culiprán peasants for social struggle and political leadership during the 1930's. "So I grew, and when I reached the age to do military service they also registered me to vote. When the election of the late Aguirre Cerda came along, the Peasant League was formed and I began to work as a leader. We were making 2.50 pesos by then, and they raised us to 3.20. When we got that raise the *patrón* axed a few of the *inquilinos* . . . They were fired for being mixed up in the Peasant League."

Two important conditions were related to the earlier peasant movements: conflict and mobilization within the farm coincided with national political mobilizations organized by insurgent, urban-based, leftist movements seeking public office. The long periods of quiescence coincided largely with periods in which the urban insurgents were holding ministerial offices, when parliamentary activity predominated, or when the laws proscribed radical political groups. Popular mobilization during the 1920 presidential election of the middle-class insurgent Arturo Alessandri was followed by agricultural policies that differed in no significant fashion from those of traditional rulers. After his election, the president and his party "demobilized" the peasantry. Repressions and isolation of the peasants returned. Contacts with urban political forces were broken; the external supports vanished. The administrative authorities continued to pursue policies buttressing the power of the landowners, who imposed quasi-absolute authority on the peasants. This pattern of rural mobilization and demobilization was repeated with little variation in the 1930's and 1940's.

Because of these reversals little if any change occurred in the status of the peasant and in the structure of authority on the farm. However, marginal gains within the farm's basic system were obtained. More important, the class struggle created a tradition that was passed on by word of mouth; experiences were shared with the younger generation; repressed demands were related to future action. This cumulative process eroded established authority. Because not all the individuals involved were eliminated, they were able to pass onto the next generation the quest for change through struggle as an alternative to the paternalistic way of problem-solving. The older peasant rebels became the storehouse of experience. Their experiences and the traditions they established legitimated the apparently nonlegitimate activity of the young militants. The eruption of violent activity ("illegal means") was not a cataclysmic event that appeared for the first time. It rested on the experience of self-mobilization and the expertise of older peasants who had been active earlier.

Contract in an Authoritarian Setting

A built-in instability accompanied each settlement that occurred within the system of owner dominance. The contract agreed to between owners and peasants in the years of peasant upsurge, whether verbal or written, was binding on the owner only so long as the movement itself lasted. Later, with the isolation of the peasantry and the reestablishment of official channels sanctioning paternal authority, the rights of the peasants and the obligations of the owners disappeared. Collective bargaining resulted at a particular moment in history when urban forces supported peasant initiatives and movements: the system of power was interdependent. Sustained self-mobilization depended on external support. Effective collective bargaining of local units, such as existed at Culiprán at certain times, appeared only when external political support countered the strength of the "right"—the administrative regulations and traditional authority of the landowners. The short duration of collective bargaining rights and the limited gains they brought did not promote peasant confidence in organizations and channels for problem-solving within the traditional structure. The failure of pragmatic reformist methods prepared the ground for attempts at more basic changes.

Culiprán's inability to institutionalize stable mechanisms for gradual change and the accumulation of experiences of class struggle within the structure of traditional authority were two major factors that led to the seizure of the farm.

Communication and Political Development

Communication with the outside world reinforced and accentuated existing sources of revolt, it did not create them. Communication with outsiders played an important role in shaping the perspective of the peasants and heightening their sense of exploitation. For example, a peasant who was a veteran of earlier struggles read in a newspaper that the government proposed an agrarian reform. He informed the other peasants. The agrarian reform project stimulated his desires and hopes for change. Interviewee One recalled an incident: "... five years ago in March we tried [to organize]. That was when I read in a paper about Alessandri's agrarian reform. I called my *compañeros* together but they didn't believe me—they never did at first. But I got them together and said: 'This is what's happening, *compañeros*, and this is what we are going to have to do.' Later we met again, and I talked to them again, and finally some believed me."[5]

While skeptical of the report that the government would actually take a hand in affairs on the farm they worked, the news activated the peasants. It encouraged them to organize, to implement what they perceived as government-sanctioned activity. In Culiprán the mass media's penetration of the farm served to stimulate latent feelings. The media encouraged the peasants to go beyond "subpolitical" desires for change; they shaped a political perspective. The mass media and the information they introduced did not create new desires so much as they aroused and reinforced existing desires, products of earlier experiences. Mass communications were one input in the process of political change, dependent on the existence of traditions and experiences that facilitated acceptance or rejection of change. The peasants of Culiprán made contact with the outside world through the small-scale commercialization of crops they raised to supplement their meager earnings as wage hands for the landowner. The revolt of the peasants against the owner resulted partly from the growth of small-scale commercial agriculture and the concomitant values of individual self-improvement. The unused land and the speculative practices of the owner aggravated a situation where the peasants, as aspiring market farmers, were confined to tiny plots, unable to fulfill their entrepreneurial desires. The seeds of revolt were present in the form of the nascent individual capitalist producers created within the *fundo*. The peasants' desire for economic expansion conflicted with the social relations and norms of the *fundo* and its restrictive structure of authority. These latent values are revealed in the comments of Interviewee One: "I've always been an *inquilino*, but I've always thought that a person could do more. What I have always wanted is to make money and have a better life. To own a little bit of land where I am boss—some money and eight cuadras to work with my sons. I already

[5] Jorge Alessandri, an independent conservative, was elected in 1958 and served until 1964, when Frei was elected.

have an opportunity because I have a friend who says that . . . he'll open an account for me in the bank." The peasant's interest in commercial exploitation of agriculture was evident by his wish to obtain machinery to assist him: "If I had a little tractor and five cuadras to work, I guarantee that, if those five cuadras are good land, then even with corn alone I can make 15 million; and if I spend five I still have ten left."[6]

Contact with the outside world was somewhat restricted. Transportation and visiting were generally limited. Those peasants who became local leaders were usually among the minority who had more frequent interaction with the outside world. The number of peasants who were isolated held less significance than the existence of a meaningful minority of peasants who carried the experiences of commercial and urban society back to their brethren in the closed system of social control.

The high proportion of peasants in Culiprán who were literate and the high percentage of eligible voters who actually cast ballots indicated the existence of an available audience for the impersonal media and for mobile political organizations.[7] The transistor radio and, less frequently, the newspaper were the media through which the generally literate peasantry became aware of the news. Nevertheless, it is important to note that the peasants interpreted the news according to their perceived needs, choosing to remember news items of particular relevance to their immediate local situation. The conservative-controlled media did not block the development of rural radicalism. The absence of many personal contacts with the outside world was no great obstacle to political mobilization. The existence of mass rural literacy, social struggles dating back to the 1920's, and mass political participation even on the minimum level of voting suggests that the traditional structure of authority was already being undermined.

The modernization favored by the owner class itself became an instrument in activating struggles that destroyed the owners' authority. The owners' decision to change from payments in kind (*regalías*) to payments in cash contributed to the politization of the peasantry. The withdrawal of traditional payments in kind was perceived by all the peasants as a threat to their daily existence. Interviewee Three underlined the importance of the loss of these perquisites in producing the peasant revolt.

---

[6] Five thousand pesos were roughly equivalent to one dollar.

[7] Most political parties confined their visits to the rural areas to pre-electoral periods, and this habit did have some effect in slowing down the pace of political mobilization.

Now I am going to tell you how it came about that the land was taken over . . . The owner, May 1 [1965], took away the traditional payments in kind [*regalías*]. He gave us one acre of land and two acres to rent. The rest was taken away. He charged us. Nine thousand pesos were to be discounted from our salary. Three thousand for a carload of firewood. And for bread we had to pay 600 pesos. Then we remained to starve. We said: What are we going to do with the family? Here we are twelve in the house, two grown-ups. We would have to starve. What were we to do with a fourth of land to clothe and sustain the family? It was not sufficient to eat. This was on payday—Saturday. Then we came together around here: This is going to happen. It's going to happen that we are going to starve. What are we going to do? Are we going to stop work on Monday? Well, we did it. All of us joined the stoppage; and we asked him to give us more payments and that he shouldn't deduct these interest payments. Nothing was done. Nothing. Nothing. So he left us on the same old terms.

The alienation of the peasant from his ancient moorings on his tiny plot of land—the attempt by the owners to rationalize one dimension of the social relations at the expense of traditional benefits—brought forth a series of counterresponses that went far beyond the original issues. Payments in cash and the charges imposed by the owner for traditional benefits made the system of mutual obligations inoperative and impersonalized relations. The peasant-owner relation became more strictly instrumental. Affective particularistic relations that served as a buffer and that tended to undermine collective demands were eliminated. Capitalist modernization and rationalization served to alienate the peasants and to activate them toward collective action.

3. The Traditional Basis of a Modern Revolt

What began as a protest against the violation of traditional norms became a challenge to the traditional structure of social control. Once the struggle broke out, the goals of the peasants changed. They were oriented not toward restoration of the old obligations but toward taking over the profit-maximizing position of the owner and establishing themselves as individual capitalist farmers. The expropriation and division of the land were the "revolutionary" means of extending and deepening the process of modernization and individuation.

The owner's practice of manipulating the marketing of produce in order to maximize profit is one aspect of his economic conduct that provoked the extreme reaction of the peasants. His capitalist emphasis on profit maximization contrasted sharply with the traditional norms he held before the peasants as ideals, and the peasants were aware of this contradiction. They mentioned that the owner stored crops and meats in order to obtain higher prices even while the peasants were hungry. The contrast between the individual gain of the owner and the social needs of the peasants was viewed by many as a particular personal vice of the owner. For the peasant leaders this contrast was instrumental in creating an awareness of the different interests of both the peasants and the owners. As the peasants pursued their self-interest in conflict with that of the owner, the farm became further polarized. Conflict revolved no longer around a return to traditional obligations and rights, but around interest politics.

Alienation and Revolt

The instability of contractual relations, the violation of traditional norms, and the covert collaboration of public officials with traditional authorities created a discontented mass available for and interested in radical change. The support of an active radical opposition created the necessary external counterweight to the official support for traditional authority. Interviewee Three expressed the growing frustration of the peasants:

> Then we went to Melipilla to seek a settlement; we went to the labor inspector, to the governor, but we didn't get results there either. Because he has bought all of them, he bought all the authorities; afterward we went to court, more of the same; we stayed in the same way, because the judge didn't rule in our favor . . . And those who were supposed to look after us, the democrats [the Christian Democrats], it must be made clear, didn't do anything; they did nothing for us. One could say that it was then that the local leadership from this *fundo* went and spoke with a socialist municipal councilman, Matías Núñez [of Melipilla].

Within the farm the relationship of forces weighed heavily in favor of numbers: an active and organized peasantry easily overcame the owner and his formal and informal clients. The structure of authority was top-heavy, insofar as final authority was concentrated in the owner; in practice, however, considerable day-to-day decision-making power was delegated among the *empleados*—the general manager (administrator), the foreman, and others. The social differences between the *empleados* and the rest of the peasants were accentuated by the higher incomes and better *regalías* that the former received. The authoritarian quasi-absolutist structure of authority, then, had as its major internal support a stratum of employee clients.

Situated in a relatively privileged status position, the *empleados* depended on the system that maintained the peasants in a subordinate position. The *empleados* espoused a traditional paternal outlook and upheld these values for reasons of self-interest—the higher economic remuneration and the social status that were their rewards. Deference to the owner was based on a sense of calculation and self-interest. By defending the prerogatives of the owner, the *empleados* were defending their own position and its privileges against the peasantry. Traditional deference was expressive and instrumental.

The values articulated by the *empleados* were largely traditional: they stressed security, dependence, obedience, "natural" inequality, and trust in the economically powerful. The values of the *empleados* blend traditional authoritarianism and the modern capitalist ethic, that is, economic pursuits involving investment in property and livestock. In practice the two sets of values were not incompatible, since traditional authoritarianism did serve as a mechanism of social control for the profitable exploitation of labor. Interviewee Six, an *empleado*, expressed the dual attitude: "A year ago this month I sold two truckloads of potatoes in Santiago. I paid one thousand pesos a sack for freight and sold two hundred sacks in February. That's why I agree with the *patrón* about the *regalías*. Even if there are others who don't have as much—who haven't risen as high—because you know that everyone has his place on the ladder. Not everyone can be the same on a *fundo*. There are privates, corporals, a sergeant, and then the colonels and so forth."

The political allegiance of the *empleados* to the owner showed during the peasant takeover, when they opposed the takeover of the farm though they dared not express their opposition in the face of the overwhelming number of peasants mobilized against them. Even after the takeover the *empleados* expressed their sympathy and support for the landowner. They continued to share his conservative political outlook and identified their superior status with the maintenance of quasi-absolutist authority. The *empleados* had improved their material position through their loyalty to traditional authority, and the owner never withheld his favors from his trusted *empleados*, who maintained the system. The owner's termination of traditional *regalías* did not affect the *empleados*. The result of differential treatment sharpened the cleavage between the *empleados* and the rest of the peasantry.

The peasants viewed *empleados* as an alien privileged stratum. During the period when peasant insurgents were planning their strategy, they refused to take the *empleados* into their confidence. The *empleados* defended the concentration of authority vested in the owner and stressed his importance in maintaining security and material benefits. An *empleado* (Interviewee Six) noted: "As for me, the *patrón* was always very good to me because we were brought up together. He's always given me all my food, and everything I have I owe to him. Why should I say anything bad about him? If some people rebelled it must be because they have something wrong with them, no? Or they don't think, or don't work and just want to take it easy."

The *empleados* deprecated the decentralized democratic politics that developed after the owner was evicted, and they stressed the "disorder" of democratic politics in comparison to the authoritarian "peace" of the previous period. Debate and discussion at public meetings were characterized by Interviewee Six as "worse than a dogfight." He went on to lament the loss of discipline and respect. While he grudgingly acknowledged the skill of government agronomists, he criticized them for not commanding more respect. The *empleados* were hostile to most changes on the farm: they attacked independent voluntary associations like the trade union as well as the independence and politization of women. One *empleado* boasted of the continuance of authoritarian patterns in his own household.

The *empleados* explain political activity by the peasants as an outgrowth of their unwillingness to work. One contrasted his personal virtues leading to "success" with the vices of the peasants and their lowly position in the following manner: "I am a Democrat, and if I voted for Frei and for Don Jorge Alessandri before him, and for Carlos Ibáñez del Campo[1] before him, it was for a reason, no? I've never failed to vote in my life. And I've given the sixteen or twenty-five votes from my family to the right. You ask me why? Because it's the most orderly and peaceful way to live. You get along better with the *patrones* who like you. So the future is easier for you—especially if you're a married man."

It is interesting to contrast the *empleado's* confidence in the benignity of the owner with the peasants' distrust and hostility. Confidence in one situation is based on the granting of substantial rewards while suspicion in the other situation is based on the violation of rights. Because he was relatively satisfied with his previous position, the *empleado* held a constricted view of possible alternative modes of organizing society. "Yes, sir, all my life [I have voted] with the Conservatives, because I saw that, if one doesn't live with the people who have money, well, who are you going to live with? You have to live with the right ones."

Political polarization and alignment largely coincided with class divisions within the *fundo*: the *empleados* sided with the owner against the peasants. The socioeconomic differences among the peasants—between the skilled workers and the poorest peasants—were less influential in shaping

[1] Carlos Ibáñez del Campo, supported by a coalition of the right and the left, was president from 1952-1958. His policies generally favored the right, and during his administration there was considerable repression of popular movements, especially after his first year in office.

their political attitudes than were their common grievances with the owner. The deprivation they suffered at the hands of the owner more than offset the particular rivalries that existed among them. The peasants perceived the transformation of social relations into cash relations as producing a general deterioration of their common situation. The change of peasants into salaried workers (the loss of property status) was a key element generating a general radicalization and providing a common basis for collective action.

In the earlier period, exploitation and inequality had produced at times overt resistance to privilege and struggle for incremental improvements. Later, the withdrawal of payments in kind was a catalytic agent that propelled the peasants toward modern ideas of self-interest and group action. Once social action was proposed, the peasants became open to the ideas of self-government and representative institutions (trade unions) that could articulate their interest. Collective self-expression was embodied in their slogan at the time of the takeover: "The land for those who work it." Personal desires became social principles. Justice, once identified with the maintenance of loyalty to a paternalistic set of obligations, was redefined in terms of the peasants' own interests.

The Politics of Escalation: From Restoration to Revolution

The initial factors contributing to the disequilibrium of the social system (the withdrawal of the traditional payments in kind and the unmet demands of the peasants) provoked a series of related actions and reactions, each in turn escalating the level of conflict, leading from a strike to the expulsion of the owner from the *fundo*. The intervention of external forces (the left) hastened this process and provided the effective support that facilitated the transition. Interviewee Seven noted:

The *patrón* we had here was the worst possible. He didn't fulfill his obligations to us. He only gave us a cuarto of land as *regalía,* and, since I was a master carpenter, I had a right to one and a half cuartos. But he only gave me one. So here I was working just one cuarto and making a tiny salary. We made 8,000 or 9,000 at most. Every month we got 7,500 pesos. We started to complain one time when Don Eduardo [Marín] held the money back because of something to do with the animals we had. That was when we got some life in us and began to protest. We called a strike here—we didn't want to work. So all that money that he'd been keeping from us was given back: some got 9,000 pesos, others 12,000.

Later he divided it equally according to the number of animals we had. He had to give all that money back.

Don Manuel Muñoz was the one who organized that movement. He's from Santiago, from Puente Alto. When could we have done it alone? Never. *Compañeros* from the Socialist party came from Melipilla later.

For most rank-and-file peasants the breakdown of paternalism was an important event in the chain that led to the revolt; most peasants had lacked a clear idea of alternatives to the existing structure of authority. Once the revolt was underway, and in the course of seizing the farm, an alternative began to crystallize: peasants began to articulate and value their independence and to form ideas of individual proprietorship. For most peasants the values of peace and security were connected with owning their own plot of land. Agreements, because they were breached more often than not, and the owner's bad faith in bargaining and negotiating produced great anxiety among the peasants. The peasants did not feel secure and repeatedly expressed their irritation with the untrustworthiness of the owner. The growth of social solidarity among the previously atomized peasants was an important outcome of their political activities. Solidarity in turn contributed to their success in achieving their goals. Those members of the work force whose actions tended to undermine solidarity were isolated and referred to in a derogatory fashion (*amarillos*—yellow).

The Civic Culture: A Postrevolutionary Phenomenon

After the peasants seized the land and the government expropriated it from the owner, there were a number of significant changes. Traditional subservience among the peasants was replaced by confidence in their own ability to direct their economic and social activities. Interviewee Twelve, for example, was indignant with CORA, the government agrarian reform agency (Corporación de la Reforma Agraria) because it considered retaining the former *empleados*. He was insistent on keeping them out: "It's only a rumor, but I've heard that they want the foreman [*capataz*] and the rest of the *empleados* to stay on. They say the CORA wants to keep them on as *empleados*. We don't have to allow that under any circumstances. We have fought for this land and we want people who work on the *fundo*. We don't want to be pushed by anyone. We're used to working and running the *fundo* ourselves now, so we're not going to accept that."

The peasants supported the idea of a new democratic authority based on the solidarity of the peasants and their involvement in directing the farm. One peasant noted:

> Now I believe that the *campesino* has to be organized because unity is the only strength the *campesino* has. He has no other strength. The unions are very important in the *fundo* because they are the worker's only defense. The political parties are also important, of course, because the help of the Congress comes through them. They helped us here and we have thanked the congressmen of the Socialist party, the Communist party, and also some from the Christian Democratic party. . . .
>
> I am the leader of the union and vice-president of the Peasant Committee. . . . The election was held this November. First they elected the heads of families and they in turn elected us by secret ballot—with a ballot box. Everything still doesn't function well in our offices, because we're just getting started, but up to now we haven't had any trouble with the members of the Peasant Committee. No serious problems. But from now on I think we are going to have problems because of this question of the *empleados*. . . . Some people—*jefes* and the like—come in from other places. We have to accept that because it's done by agreements [*escrituras*] so that there's nothing anybody can do. And since the *escrituras* are the law, we are all in agreement. All of us are united and we know we have rights.

Despite their militant solidarity and sympathy for the Socialists and Communists, most of the peasants were eager to divide the land. Justice was equated with each individual's proving his worth in the market place. One peasant stated: "Yes, we're better off now, since the takeover of the land. I would have liked it if I'd had a good *patrón* like the one on San Manuel. One lives well there, with *regalías.* But it's better to have a parcel of your own. That way the lazy ones don't make anything, but if you aren't lazy and have a good piece of land you can even work at night. You have to keep working—each one on his own land."[2]

The militant peasant in Culiprán combined militancy, revolutionary activity, and pragmatic support for Socialist politicians with the goal of establishing a private capitalist enterprise. Peasant political activity in this case thus defied the usual categories of conservative/radical.

---

[2] San Manuel is a nearby farm. The owner maintained a very paternalistic system and had the general reputation of being quite generous with his peasants.

Are Peasants A "Revolutionary Class"?

The gains of the peasantry, recognized by the government's legal expropriation of the Culiprán farm, can be viewed from several angles. In terms of the immediate events, peasant participation in a confrontation and struggle in close collaboration with Marxist political leaders had a decidedly radicalizing effect on their political thinking. Nevertheless, it is not altogether certain that this is a lasting commitment—for a number of reasons. (1) The peasants showed themselves to be quite pragmatic and expressed considerable flexibility in shifting from one party to another whenever it was expedient. Hence, while many claimed to have voted for Frei, they later turned to the Socialists and may revert once again to the Christian Democrats if circumstances warrant it.[3] (2) The postexpropriation period involves the peasants in close working relationships with the government agrarian reform officials. If the relationships are perceived as beneficial, the peasants could turn to the government party. (3) Probably most important of all is the long-term economic orientation of the peasants. The peasants who were most militant and aggressive in their behavior against the landlord—those peasants who were strongest in their praise for the Socialist senator who supported them—tended also to have the strongest desire to develop commercial agricultural enterprises. Hence, if the PDC (Christian Democratic) government provides the resources to allow these entrepreneurial proclivities to take hold, the result could eventually be the embourgeoisment of the once socialistically inclined peasants.

The mobilized and politicized land-hungry peasant is a revolutionary force in society. However, once the land is distributed, the outlook of the peasants begins to shift: they continue to support those who facilitated the reform but they also look to those political forces that can preserve or expand their newly gained economic resources. The timing of change is of crucial importance in considering the process of peasant politicization. During the period of struggle for land the peasantry shows all the outward appearances of a revolutionary class (resort to violence and rejection of legal authorities); the peak of peasant radicalism occurs with the displacement of the landlord, the destruction of the old structure of authority, and the redistribution of property. The action that leads to the peasants' displacing the landlord is a revolutionary act in the sense that one social class replaces another—albeit in our account this takes place on one farm.

[3] See the Epilogue for our follow-up study six years later. The results seem to confirm our earlier observations.

Nevertheless, the locus of political power shifted drastically from the single owner and his administrative apparatus to the collective organization of the peasantry. The subsequent manner in which the national political structure responds to the internal shift in power will determine the degree to which the revolutionary movement will be absorbed into the national political structure or remain a base of support for the radical political opposition.

In sum, once politicization of the peasantry has occurred, the direction remains a problematic factor depending on external events and movements. While a politicized peasantry provides a substantial amount of raw energy and militancy through locally organized activity, its ultimate success rests with its ability to tie in with national political structures. The ability of urban-class-based parties to facilitate changes in the countryside will increase their support among a peasantry in search for change; the peasantry is by nature neither revolutionary nor accomodational: its political allegiance is dependent upon the specific types of organizations, leaders, and actions that aid it in resolving the problems posed by the landlords—in particular the problem of land redistribution.

4. The Process of Political Change

The idea of a new structure of authority appeared when the peasant became politically aware of leftist ideas and developed new political values. The growth of interest groups and class organizations indicated that new sources of legitimacy were emerging to challenge the previous structure in which only a landholder with quasi-absolute power of arbitration could authorize the granting or denial of benefits. This monarchic model represented the old system of quasi-absolute authority. The development of a compensating mechanism in the form of peasant organizations able to bargain effectively for benefits represented a challenge to this authority, though within the existing social system of the *fundo*.

At least seven distinct phases may be pointed out in the process of breakdown of the old forms of authority and establishment of new ones: (1) nearly absolute authority, (2) social differentiation and collective demands, (3) organized opposition and informal social organization, (4) conflict and confrontation, (5) attempts to restore old authority patterns, (6) reaction and revolution, and (7) establishment of the new authority. On Culiprán, each phase was reflected in the social relations between the landowner and the peasants.

In the first phase—that of nearly absolute authority—the owner dealt directly and individually with the peasants. When a *campesino* asked for redress of injustices, he did so by appealing to the charity or personal virtues of the landowner, who enjoyed complete power to decide whether to accept or reject the individual's personal request. The relationship between the landowner and the isolated peasant was therefore characterized by a near monopoly of power on the part of the landowner: the relationship is clearly authoritarian.

In the second phase, the principal sociopolitical change was the appearance of demands dealing with problems that affected all or many of the *campesinos*. These collective petitions indicated that the atomization of the peasantry (in contrast to the landowner's monopoly of power) had been partially overcome. As in previous efforts, the peasants became aware of their common plight and made their demands collectively. The peasants perceived a weakening of the repressive apparatus—a Christian Democratic government. They were conscious that collective action might be more likely to produce positive results.

The third phase, organized opposition, was characterized by the establishment of an informal committee that began to assume the responsibility of looking out for the interests of the peasants. This committee offered to the *campesino* a visible alternative source of authority, and it therefore represented the nucleus of a developing crisis of dual authority on the *fundo*. The decisions of the landowner were no longer accepted passively, but were discussed and evaluated according to the *campesinos'* own perceptions of their interests. Decisions contrary to these interests were criticized, and the exchange of opinions within the informal group became the basis for the formation of a more clearly defined expression of group interest.

The fourth phase, conflict and confrontation, was characterized by the confrontation of forces—the landowners and the informally organized peasants—in open disagreement over the decisions to be made. The struggle manifested itself in a sharp sociopolitical polarization, and the independently organized peasant forces graduated from informal encounters to true meetings. Attendance at these meetings was restricted to the peasants, who made decisions about the course of events and strategy. The breakdown of the *fundo* over the relationship between the owner and the peasantry created a duality of powers in the decision-making process. In the absence of a clear delimitation of authority, negotiations were sterile, and the emerging forces exercised their authority through a peasant strike, which paralyzed the workings of the *fundo*. The deepening crisis of authority was made clear by the fact that the old authority (the owner) could no longer count on an obedient work force. Still, these new activities remained within the old framework of labor and property. There were no parallel changes in the sources of authority, that is, in the possession and use of the chief material resources: the land, production, and the machinery.

In the fifth stage the landowner recovered from the impact of the initial challenge and tried to reestablish his absolute authority. By attempting to deal directly with individuals, and especially by offering certain benefits, he intended to return to the stage of individual requests that preceded unionization. This attempt by the landowner to undermine the new relationship was based on the supposition that it was merely a passing phenomenon caused by momentary necessities or problems. This was a dangerous evaluation of the problem because of the socially explosive consequences of the landowner's crude attempts to strengthen his traditional absolute power. The landowner's commitment to traditional forms thus became a prelude to revolt.

Naturally, the new and unstable definitions of authority and power never served as a basis for the calculations of the landowner. The irritating coexistence imposed by the signing of a legal contract was broken. The landowner, incapable of understanding the new power structure and the weakening of his own authority, or unwilling to admit to them, failed to meet the contractual conditions of work and remuneration. The failure of his attempt to restore the old system and undermine the new authority through compensations to chosen groups and individuals led the landowner to seek to drive up the costs of the new organizations. Breaking with the paternalism inherent in his authority, the landowner tried to cut back on the payments in kind (*regalías*) that were a part of the traditional system of payment.

To the *campesinos* this extreme example of arbitrary confiscation (*despojo*) occurred just as the experience of organizing and participating in political activity had increased their confidence and self-esteem. Aware of their ability to deal effectively with the owner, they came to consider him arbitrary in his methods and incompetent to manage the *fundo*. From questioning the authority of the landowner to decide questions relating to their salaries, they began to think of the *fundo* itself as a means of betterment. The owner's violation of the pact created a deeper distrust among the *campesinos* and strengthened their sense of social solidarity. This, together with the attempt to take away their traditional payments in kind, brought the end of the tense coexistence characteristic of the period of dual power.

The sixth period—that of reaction and revolution—saw the landowner's attempt to reestablish the values and norms of the old authority structure in the new situation. Opposed to him was the *campesinos'* attempt to broaden their authority to include greater material possessions. The landowner's imposition of new expenses served as a catalyst.

Those peasants who were prepared for the struggle by previous experiences assumed the leadership of the movement. In the new situation the oldest extremists became the spark that ignited the larger group of *campesinos*.

Dissatisfaction with the instability of the system of dual authority, and with the inability to negotiate or define new and mutually satisfactory relations, led the *campesinos* to try to eliminate the obstruction—the landowner. The initial impulse of the movement—social and economic progress within the *fundo* and the peasants' recognition of their legal right to make contracts—made the meaning of the occupation of the *fundo* somewhat ambiguous. Was the takeover merely a means to pressure the owner, or was it done with the goal of expropriation? The existence of a president elected after promising "100,000 new landowners in 6 years," the presence of government organizations (CORA, INDAP) equipped to bring about the expropriation of lands, and a national atmosphere impregnated by "agrarian reformism" all contributed to the peasant's feeling of legality and rightness about the occupation of the *fundo*. Social necessities, personal desires, and legality were mutually reinforcing and were expressed by the decisiveness and conviction of the peasants. When confronted by *carabineros* (national police), they refused to give up the land, for once the lands were occupied the process of political transformation seemed to them irreversible. They felt prepared to dispense with the owner and run the *fundo* themselves.

The seventh stage of "the new authority" followed the expulsion of the owner. The decision-making process on the *fundo* was reorganized as a mixture of direct democracy and representative institutions. After the expropriation, the *campesinos* considered the new situation to be a qualitative step forward, but they were not convinced of its security. They shared their decision-making power with the government, and resorted to state organizations for credit and technical aid. The period of transition was to be passed under a structure halfway between immediate division of the land and collectivization; the *campesinos* formed a "committee of *asentamiento*" to work the *fundo* collectively for three years. At the end of the period the definitive decision would be made as to whether the land should be collectively administered or divided up.

This new authority structure based on popular participation—either direct or through general assemblies—was reflected in the peasants' attitudes in four general areas: the rural society, themselves, their work, and the future.

In their attitudes toward rural society, the *campesinos*, especially the leaders, tended to generalize their own experience and advocate the general substitution of the old authority by the new social forces in ascension—the peasantry. This attitude had its share of vagueness, especially among the less politicized *campesinos*, who saw the problem as one of "good" and "bad" owners. There was also a tendency of the peasants to extend their own desires of change to the *campesinos* of the region, and to believe that others would also be able to reach the desired goal (expropriation) if they showed as much initiative and group cohesiveness as the Culiprán peasantry. They conceived of rural society in dynamic terms and felt that conflict and peasant activism should play an important role in the establishment of a new system of authority.

In their attitudes toward themselves, the *campesinos* felt secure and capable of dealing with problems and political questions—particularly those relating to the management of the *fundo*. Previously, their role in the countryside had been characterized by servility, resignation, and impotence; but as these attitudes disappeared, an optimistic one de eloped toward the future and the possibility of social and economic progress within the rural society. Work came to be seen as a means to achieve positive ends without the stigma of social inferiority or economic privation that it had carried under the old system. The new structure of authority, the introduction of popular democracy, and the considerable control over the decision-making process were decisive factors in the formation of these new attitudes—valuable ingredients in the process of social and economic development.

Throughout the period of growth of the new peasant organization, the *campesinos* sought external help in dealing with their problems. At the beginning they appealed for governmental-bureaucratic support of petitions to force the owner to observe his legal obligations to them. The owner's noncompliance with the laws and the inability of local bureaucrats to employ force against him were factors that caused the peasant leaders to turn to the support of radical groups. The impotence of the local labor inspectors in the face of the *campesinos'* most fundamental problems deepened the discontent and frustration of the peasants. They became ripe for political mobilization in defiance of the existing authority.

The "outside" peasant leaders, especially those at the national level, were important in making the local struggle a national issue. The peasants' ability to use the support of national political leaders against the land-owner played an important part in the outcome of the struggle.

The national peasant leaders furnished aid in the form of ideas about organization, tactical and strategic planning, and national publicity. Though it is difficult to determine to what extent these external forces contributed to deciding the course of events in each stage of the process, the interviews indicate that it was considerable. External help, then, played an important role in facilitating the successful occupation of the *fundo*. The situation on the hacienda was thus resolved by decisions taken at the national level by the government and the national political agents of the peasantry.

This mutual interaction between the internal struggle and external support was the key to the success of the takeover. If the *campesinos* succeeded in tearing down the local authority structure, it was because they were able to mobilize political resources effectively at the national level. The specific relation of powers at the national level favored the emergence of a new structure of authority at the local level, and the landowner could no longer identify the retention of his own authority with the authority of the national government.

Peasant Politicization and National Politics

The growth of peasant politicization coincided with periods during which political mobilization of insurgent popular groups was occurring on the national political scene. The relationships between peasant activism and the national political structure is complex and dialectical: a number of levels of analysis will reveal that at one time or another each sector provided the energy to stimulate the other to action.

Among peasants it is possible to isolate prepolitical feelings, reflecting traditional and customary beliefs transmitted by word of mouth, that express the repressed or latent demands activated by internal changes on the farm or by urban forces. Latent demands and prepolitical feelings toward landownership and landlord exploitation were underlying ingredients present in the politicization of the peasantry. Personal contacts, market relationships, and the media—mostly urban-based sources of influence—encouraged the peasants to articulate overtly their needs in the form of demands.

Peasant activity in turn became a pressure on urban political groups and stimulated competition among the reform oppositionist groups seeking supporters. They in turn offered their services to the peasants: petitions were written and presented, grievances were publicized, public officials were confronted. The peasants consciously manipulated political spokesmen of the competing groups, attempting to locate the most effective political agency for accomplishing their ends. The competition of Marxist and Christian Democratic parties for the allegiance of the peasantry gave the latter for the first time in history an opportunity to play off one group against another in the hopes of coming out on top.

In previous periods revolts were initially encouraged by urban groups and then later abandoned; in the present period a new set of factors in national politics has partially altered this situation: (1) The 1964 election campaign was largely between two candidates who rallied support on the basis of a comprehensive agrarian reform. The publicity and public response were so overwhelming that it would have been very difficult to back away from some positive public action; at the very least the government was forced to adopt a less overtly partisan use of coercive forces at the behest of the propertied landed elite. In the first years of the Frei government it was difficult to send police to dislodge peasants who were only doing what the president had promised a thousand times. Nevertheless, on more than one occasion the president did send in the troops. However, the PDC, unlike past governments, was forced by national politics to recognize some illegal peasant actions (similar to the takeover described here) as having some legitimacy. (2) Within the Christian Democratic party and government there was a deep cleavage between the right wing (including President Frei) and the left wing (led by Jacques Chonchol). The agrarian reform program was partially under the leadership of left-wingers like Chonchol, who encouraged peasant organization. Chonchol was largely instrumental in creating the permissive climate in rural areas and in neutralizing the repressive propensities of the right wing of the party. (3) Alongside the profound division within the government party there was a large active Marxist urban and peasant movement that provided resources and support to peasant social action, thus contributing to the process of peasant politicization. Thus, both the left-wing Christian Democrats in the government and the Marxist opposition outside the government were able to neutralize the repressive efforts of the liberal-democratic state and in many cases to provide new channels through which peasant demands could be expressed and even realized.

Problematics of the Study of Peasant Political Consciousness

Some questions arise relating to the nature of the events that occur when *fundos* are taken over. Is the takeover of lands a symptom of genuine pressure applied by the peasants? Is this pressure the result of a peasant consciousness, or is it impossible to make generalizations about consciousness in crisis situations because they are the products of peculiar conditions that do not exist to the same degree on all *fundos*? To put it in more general terms: is the takeover caused by a constellation of conditions that are not common to the peasantry as a whole and that are not influenced by peasant consciousness? Questions like these lead to others of equal significance that urgently require answers. What is the peasantry? Is it a class? What is meant by peasant consciousness and the maturation of peasant consciousness? Do all *campesinos* share a common predicament? What is meant by solidarity among peasants? Is there a difference between the peasant and the agricultural worker? Is the peasant's condition different than that of the industrial worker?

Countless measures have been taken to bring the peasant into political life. The peasant is the focus of technical and political discussions and the battlefield on which pressure groups struggle for power. To many, the peasants are the group destined to give the final blow that causes the collapse of the dominant socioeconomic regime, and the struggle to organize them revolves around the hope that they will express an authentic desire for change. Agrarian reform is the process that speaks to their strongest desires, and its success depends entirely on their ability to take collective action. Nevertheless, we do not intend to approach these complex considerations without stopping to tackle the simple questions raised earlier. These and many other questions can only be answered by a clarification of the true nature of the consciousness possessed by the peasant groups involved in political movements.

Our approach can be summed up in the following points:

1. Analysis of external factors and their impact within the *fundo*. We begin with the hypothesis that the more open the system is to the influence of these factors, the greater the likelihood of the development of consciousness among the *campesinos*.

2. Study of the dynamic internal factors operating within the system

and their impact on the development of a trade union or political consciousness. Our hypothesis is that the broader the system of interactions, the greater the possibilities of the development of a peasant consciousness.

3. Analysis of social relations within the *fundo*: the solidarity of different social groups, the exchange of services, the functional division of work. Finally, the relation of these aspects with the uneven development of a trade union or political consciousness.

The stages in the formation of consciousness are then analyzed according to the following breakdown:

1. Consciousness subjected to the paternalism of the owner.

2. Trade union consciousness subjected to paternalism, in which the external factors of support are a function of the dominant paternalism.

3. Autonomous social consciousness. The peasantry uses its power as a work force to challenge the owner's authority within the limits of the system.

4. Autonomous political consciousness. The peasants are now considered an authority group. At this stage the limits of the system are transcended and a broader social horizon is opened.

Finally, it should be clear that these aspects serve only as a reference frame for the analysis, and at no time will they limit us if the empirical data suggest new alternatives of analysis. It is to assure this contact with reality and to avoid limiting reality with restrictive hypotheses that the technique of participant observation and the semistructured interview have been chosen. These precautions are the more important when the object of the study is such an unknown.

Social Interaction and Social Change

The social, economic, and political description of the *fundo* should be complemented with a description of the characteristics of the estate as a system of interactions. This aspect is very important for understanding the *fundo's* internal dynamics.

Since the change of the agrarian structure is expressed concretely in modifications of the system of tenancy, it is useful to know what impact this change has on the structure of the peasant group itself. For in fact, peasant behavior sometimes presupposes modifications of the tenancy system that are not clearly expressed institutionally. The most important of these changes is the separation or dissociation of the economic function and the power function within the tenancy system. Of course this dissociation is closely linked to the nature of the dominant groups of the society.

If agriculture is replaced as the basic support of these groups by other more dynamic economic activities, the functions assigned to the system of tenancy will be affected. If new groups actually replace the traditional landowning class, the loss of the power function will be much more profound than if an alliance of sectors is established or if the change is restricted to a simple broadening of the activities of the farmers who have effectively held power. Thus, the dissociation of the power function in the agrarian system is conditioned by the nature of the dominant group.

Urban-rural relations are also important factors regarding the nature of these groups because they represent the other aspect of the equilibrium between the sectors. The balance, or lack of it, in the development of the mode of production means that in urban-rural relations one sector may come to be dependent upon or complementary to the other. It is most important, however, to determine to what point the structure of the dominant groups is a cause or a symptom of this imbalance. The question hinges on whether the dominant group is solely a landowning class or is allied with industrial groups that may be either independent or the "byproducts" of the landowners' activity in the industrial sector. It is also possible that the dominant group may be solely industrial, but this study will limit itself to the changes in the tenancy system produced by modifications in urban-rural relations. It does not deal with the other related processes.

We have restricted our study of this problem to the following questions: (1) what influences do urban-rural relations have on the system of tenancy? (2) through what channels do these influences reach the peasantry? (3) what are the effects of the process upon the peasant class itself? Our hypothesis is that when the system of tenancy fulfills a function of power at the same time that it furnishes the support of economic activity (as in the traditional hacienda), it is characterized by isolation—the most important basis of paternalistic power relations. Any circumstance that alters the situation affects this power—if not in its very structure, at least in its underpinnings. Such an alteration requires new forms of legitimization capable of conserving the worker-*patrón* relationship. In other words: when the system of tenancy loses its power function because of a breach in isolation, there arises a need for new relations, the nature of which will ultimately be determined by the importance of agriculture as a power base at the national level. At this stage of the restructuring of power bases, the peasant undergoes transformations that affect the nature of emerging relations. Because of the implications for agrarian change, it is most interesting to determine when and how a new mentality begins to develop among the agricultural workers, and it is especially important to pinpoint the actual moment of the crisis reflected by the loss of the power function and the consequent changes in the nature of the dominant group.

Isolation can be broken by different means that reflect different changes in the society as a whole.

Value Integration: Value integration is the process of universalizing the aspirations shared by the population of a country regardless of urban, rural, or other social considerations. The phenomenon takes place because of the rapid growth of the mass media and increased physical mobility. The result is the narrowing or disappearance of cultural distances. Value integration is also produced by all forms of urban penetration in rural areas: education, commercial relations, union organization, politics. All these factors and processes tend to integrate rural and urban values and to minimize their differences. On the structural level, of course, a greater measure of differentiation persists.

This process of rural-urban integration is obviously important in the development of the peasant consciousness. It constitutes a dynamic element within the agrarian system, for it creates the preconditions necessary to produce the qualitative change that occurs when the tenancy system is no longer able to continue using the old mechanisms for holding back the peasantry.

The Breakdown of the Traditional System. When the traditional system of tenancy is no longer able to continue to function on the basis of a permanent work force tied to the *fundo* by such mechanisms as the *regalía*, and a gap is opened between what the system demands and what it can produce, the conditions that make the rules of the paternalistic system acceptable disappear. This change gives rise to a conflict situation within the limits of the system. The breakdown of isolation through value integration, however, eases the transformation of the *campesinos* into an authority group competing with the patronal authority in the conflict situation.

Urban-rural integration and the breakdown of the traditional system are the processes that move most rapidly toward the transformation of the tenancy system. Both express the contradiction between the traditional agrarian structure and a new value structure that is no longer solely the reflection of agrarian activity. The new structure of values is the result of an urban influence and a greater degree of value integration between city and country, which fosters change even in the absence of development.

Still other agents for the transformation of the tenancy system may be found in the activities of the landowners themselves. In this case the change of the system comes about because of the adoption of new relations and functions by the owner group; whereas in the previous case change occurs because the tenancy system finds itself in conflict with new realities that destroy its base of support.

5. The Integration of Agrarian Activity in the Larger Socioeconomic Context

When agriculture ceases to be a primary activity separated from other forms of production, it incorporates itself vertically into the economic structure along the lines of industrial organization. The landowner does not merely undergo change—he initiates it by integrating his agricultural activities with the commercial and industrial spheres.

The breakdown of isolation leads to alterations of power relationships and the tenancy system because of the change in the structure of the owner group. Of course, when landowners also engage in other economic activities, the ownership of land loses its importance as a power base. In such cases, the power base shifts to other, more dynamic, sectors, and agriculture—stripped of its noneconomic functions of prestige, security, and power—becomes only a profitable activity.

The case under study offers some other possibilities. In order for agriculture to cease to fulfill an important power function, it is not necessary for it to be integrated into complexes like those earlier mentioned: agriculture may lose its power factor simply because power passes to other sectors, or the process may be reversed and business or industrial interests may establish links with agriculture. When the latter is the case, the norms of agrarian organization show a striking urban influence, which further contributes to the breakdown of the system's isolation.

Our study of the *fundo* Culiprán is approached in terms of isolation and the process that has contributed to the breakdown of this isolation. In order to understand the mechanisms that caused the breakdown, it is necessary to consider the characteristics of Culiprán that are relevant to the process of value integration and the imbalance of the traditional system.

The process of value integration may be approached from different angles. To begin, the physical dimension of relations with the outside must be kept in mind: whether the *campesinos* are near a population center or whether they are served by transportation that allows them to go to other parts of the province or country. In this sense, Culiprán is favorably located. The hacienda is only twelve kilometers from the town of Melipilla (25,000 inhabitants). The road is paved and collective public transportation is available once a day. In addition to these facilities, 39 percent of the peasants have their own means of transportation (wagons, buggies, or bicycles), and 1 percent possess motor vehicles. The rest of the population has no private means of transportation.

Because of this situation—and because such transportation as bicycles and vehicles without the necessary draft animals are considered in the transportation figures—the peasants do not have the option of taking their harvests to town to be sold. They must depend, therefore, on the buyers who come to the hacienda to purchase produce, or they must pay the freight charges to have their produce trucked to the city. This situation is important in measuring the *campesinos'* possibilities of interaction with others. For if they themselves market their products locally, they have the chance of making contact with different types of individuals in the town, and consequently they become familiar with and assimilate values and standards of conduct different from those of the hacienda. The *campesinos* of Culiprán did not have this opportunity, though they did have contact with buyers who came to the *fundo*.

The fact that in Culiprán the network of social relations was not extended by the selling of produce did not preclude other forms of contact. The mass media were of limited importance. The use of the radio, for instance, is very common; more than 53 percent of the population owns a radio, while another 22 percent without private radios hear programs in the homes of neighbors or friends. Only 25 percent of the population neither owns a radio nor listens to programs. Political news is the preferred programming, followed by musical programs and, finally, sports events. But contact with the mass media is not limited to the radio. Newspapers are read by 60.2 percent (80 families) at least once every fifteen days, while 39.8 percent (53 families) do not read newspapers at all. The percentage of those who read magazines is 38.3 percent, leaving 61.7 percent who do not.

These data, however, are not sufficient to allow us to draw conclusions about the level of effective participation by the population of Culiprán in national society. We must know something of the peasant's capacity to accept information before we can determine mass media's power to introduce new frames of reference. We must examine the peasant's educational level and his participation in activities that permit him to gain a richer experience than if he is limited exclusively to his work within the *fundo*. Statistics show that 71.2 percent of the men and 75.1 percent of the women of Culiprán are literate, and the majority (men, 55.4%; women, 61.6%) have reached between the fourth and sixth year of secondary schooling. These figures are considerably superior to the national average for peasants. This high literacy rate, together with the strong tendency to buy and read newspapers, shows that the *campesinos* are capable of receiving and understanding "messages" from outside the *fundo*, which intensifies the process of acculturation and value integration.

Receptivity to cultural stimuli is shown in certain forms of participation, such as political activity. Of the 61.9 percent of the population that is registered to vote, 92.6 percent actually do exercise the franchise. Receptivity is likewise expressed by participation in the union of *fundo* workers and in such organizations as the sports club. When a *campesino* participates in the electoral process and comes into contact with ideas, programs, leaders, and other persons outside the narrow world of the *fundo*, he becomes part of a broader system of social interaction than that of the other peasants.

In spite of his participation in organizations that help him to overcome the limits of the *fundo*, however, the peasant's personal relations with the outside world (Table 13) are few because of his tendency toward endogamy. Interpersonal relations outside the system of the *fundo* are relatively less important than involvement through the mass media. The places most visited are urban centers to which some child or relative has emigrated. This aspect of interaction with the outside may be defined as "active" because initiative is implied in the act of leaving the *fundo*. But if it is compared with the relatively "passive" receiving of visitors from outside (Table 14), the pattern does not change significantly.

It is clear, then, that the peasants' system of interactions is virtually

TABLE 13

Families Who Make Visits to Other Centers

Once a week	2.3%	
Once every two weeks	5.3%	
Once a month	18.3%	23.6%
Once every 2 to 4 months	9.8%	
Once every 6 months	3.7%	
Once a year	20.3%	
Less than once a year	2.3%	60.2%
Never	37.6%	

Grouping these figures according to frequency:

Frequently visit other centers	26.4%	
Rarely visit other centers	33.8%	73.7%
Never visit other centers	39.9%	

Source: Edy Ferreira C., Alberto Peña M., Raquel Ugarte V., *Descripción de una Comunidad en Proceso de Cambio: Culiprán* (Santiago: ICIRA, 1969).

TABLE 14

Families Receiving Visitors from Other Centers

Once a week	1.5%	
Frequently (once every two weeks)	4.5%	
Once a month	5.3%	9.8%
Every two to four months	14.3%	
Rarely (every six months)	8.3%	
Once a year	33.0%	
Less than once a year	0.8%	66.9%
Never	33.1%	

Grouping these figures according to frequency:

Frequently receive visitors	11.3%	
Rarely receive visitors	55.6%	89.5%
Never receive visitors	33.9%	

Source: Ferreira et al., *Descripción*.

limited to the population of the *fundo*. To further emphasize this point, we can analyze forms of contact that do not assume a dimension of physical mobility. In a rural population with a relatively high degree of literacy, for example, such an analysis might focus on correspondence sent and received (Table 15).

Letters are generally sent to the same places to which visits are made. It seems evident that, even in cases where some sort of social relations are established with the outside, these are of relatively small importance and geographically localized. This lack of outside contact can be underscored by analyzing the frequency with which peasants receive letters from their relatives or friends who live outside the *fundo* (Table 16). Taken as a whole, these figures show the contrast between the limited system of personal relations and the broad peasant participation in the system of mass communications, indicating the direction that these relations may take in the future.

TABLE 15

Families That Send Letters to Other Centers

Once a week	1.5%
Frequently (every two weeks)	3.0%
Once a month	12.0%
Every two to four months	18.0%
Rarely (every six months)	7.5%
Once a year	7.5%
Less than once a year	0.9% } 58.0%
Never	49.6%

Grouping these figures according to frequency:

Frequently send letters	16.5%
Rarely send letters	33.0%
Never send letters	50.5%

Source: Ferreira et al., *Descripción*.

TABLE 16

Families That Receive Letters

Frequently receive letters	14.7%
Rarely receive letters	38.2% } 85.0%
Never receive letters	46.8%

Source: Ferreira et al., *Descripción*.

Santiago is the center most frequented by peasants from Culiprán, followed by Melipilla (the nearest town). In third place are some other rural centers situated on the road to Santiago; in fourth place (exceptionally and for very special reasons), Viña and Valparaíso; in fifth place are the neighboring *fundos*; and, finally, other outlying urban centers.

The conclusion to be drawn is that there is practically no personal interrelation between the populations of local or neighboring *fundos*. The *fundo* populations live in nearly total isolation from each other and are more oriented toward the mass media and urban centers with which they feel some identity through emigrant relatives who live there. It is interesting to note this social vacuum between the system and its immediate surroundings, for it may be of fundamental importance in impeding the development of a group social consciousness among the peasantry of a given region. The phenomenon may give rise to a kind of group aristocracy—a tendency to become a "reference group" for the other peasants with whom no feeling of solidarity develops. The result may be a proud feeling of exclusiveness by the newly powerful.

The value integration that can be achieved through the diffusion of the mass media does not contribute very directly to the broadening of the *campesino*'s system of social relations. This dual process may mean that politization, for instance, is taking place on two levels: The first level consists of formal political values (activity in certain political parties) in which the peasant can adopt slogans and follow leaders while his attitudes and behavior remain within the traditional framework as though those values did not exist. A second level of politization may occur when the traditional system is in crisis and the peasant sees no reason to adapt himself to it. In this case the *campesino* seeks new alternatives, which may lead in different directions but do not exclude the possibility of reviving the traditional system of relations after the crisis has passed.

On the other hand, it may be said that the value integration made possible by mass media begins a process of cultural change that eventually modifies the *campesino*'s system of interactions. It breaks down isolation and intensifies the pressures on the traditional structure, and the tendency to emigrate, while undermining the foundations of the power relations founded in isolation.

Value integration alone cannot transform the peasant into a protagonist of change within the system unless there is a parallel growth of his own system of interactions—a break with the isolation that reinforces all his dependent relations. It is only after this break that the assimilation of new values may go beyond simple formalism or functional adaptation. Nor will the process take place if the hacienda has not entered into crisis, so that it becomes impossible for the peasant to use the system of mutual obligations and duties to satisfy the interests that he has defined for himself. Value integration, then, is not in itself sufficient to open and weaken the system if it does not have the foundation of an objective broadening of the *campesino*'s system of interactions and an ever decreasing ability of the system to satisfy the peasant's needs.

The broadening of the system of interaction permits value integration to define less paternalistic types of behavior without upsetting the status quo and the structure of worker-*patrón* relations. It is the system's incapacity to satisfy the peasant's most overt pressures that sets up the conditions in which the status quo may be challenged. It is necessary to remember, however, that even in this situation, the peasant's behavior can still be determined by motivations that do not differ basically from those he experienced as a worker on the hacienda. Value integration and the process of acculturation do not change the structure of values, but they can redefine the structure into which the values of the old hacienda system are fit. A change in values may take place after this redefinition, but before it occurs, the only effect of the opening of the system is the reinforcement of the peasant's condition—though in a modified situation that does not impose the same restrictions as the hacienda. Let us look briefly at the case of Culiprán in light of these considerations.

6. Crisis in the System: The Declining Influence and Prestige of the *Patrón*

It is interesting to note the material conditions in which the peasants of the *fundo* lived and worked, for they constitute the backdrop against which the process of value integration contributes to the opening of the system and the adoption of the desire to take the land.

In general, the peasants' conditions on the *fundo* were deplorable. The landowner paid less than the minimum wage prescribed by law and acted arbitrarily in his dealings with peasants. In response to a law establishing a minimum salary, the owner restricted the traditional *regalías* from one-half cuadra (2 acres) to one-fourth cuadra and demanded rent for the rest (ten escudos per month). He also demanded payment for the pasturage of the livestock the *campesinos* kept on the hacienda (nine escudos per animal), charged three escudos for each cartload of firewood, and 0.60 escudos for the bread, water, and other necessities of the peasantry. In addition to changing the *regalía* into another source of income, the landowner required that each house have an *obligado* and a *voluntario* (day laborer). If the peasants did not comply, they were allowed to keep their homes only on a loan basis. "I've been like this for a year because I signed on as an *obligado*—I was to answer for the house. But last year my father left and they took the house away from me. They loaned it to me without rights to the land and with half of the field to plant and without livestock."

Eighteen *inquilinos* were in these conditions. Other *campesinos* claimed that "the cuarto of land they gave was the worst land—it wasn't enough to live on." "What can be produced from the *regalías* isn't enough to sell, there's only enough for our consumption. The land they give is bad—it's only good for potatoes and corn."

These responses suggest that the system of mutual obligations and responsibilities did not work on the hacienda. Conditions were such that the *inquilinos* were not receiving the right to cultivate their own pieces of land in return for the work they performed. The *inquilino* was subject to an exploitative relationship with no compensation.

It is not difficult to understand the image that the *campesinos* had of the owner. "He [the *patrón*] made a joke out of it when we showed him a biscuit that he gave us—it was really bad, filthy. 'This is the kind of biscuit you give us, *patrón*,' we said, and we gave it to him. He took it and started to eat it, then he said, 'If a fly fell into your plate of stew you'd rather throw out the stew than eat the fly'. . . . That was how he made a joke out of it when we presented our complaints . . ." Another *campesino* said: "The *patrón* we had here was the worst possible. He didn't fulfill his obligations to us. . . . If you went to ask him for a favor . . . he would say, 'How can I loan you the money if I don't have any?' . . . Then he'd turn his pockets inside out . . ." Another informant gave further evidence of the worker's negative image of the *patrón* when he said: "He abused us. Instead of giving the meat of the animals that died to the workers, he sold it to the butchers in Melipilla without any sanitary control. And if the rats had already eaten the meat, he piled them [the bones] up in the storehouses to wait for a good price for them. Some bones have been there for thirty years." The owner's greed also led him to "store five thousand sacks of wheat in the warehouse—rotting for two years while he waited for a high price—and if he caught some *inquilino* grabbing a handful of corn he'd fire him."

Other informants referred to the owner's indifference toward the initiatives of the workers. The peasants had a sports club, "but the *patrón* never gave them any help—not even so much as small change for the club." It is not surprising that this indifference also extended to more personal questions—to the worker-*patrón* relations so important to the peasant oriented by the protective image of the *patrón*. "As for Marín, the *patrón*, his main defect was that he was one of the worst *patrones* in Chile. . . . he never came around at Easter or at New Years, or even during the year to ask: 'How are my *inquilinos*? Is there anything you need?' Never. Just rules and politeness and more rules while he took away from us whatever he could." The owner did not fit the peasants' image of the traditional *patrón*, whose own demands can be met as long as he fulfills his part of the system of mutual obligations. "If the *patrón* isn't a good one, you don't have much security."

Nevertheless, this negative image of an arbitrary and avaricious *patrón* was not generalized to include all other landowners. On this level, not even the most highly politicized element of the *fundo* has overcome the social borders of the hacienda: those peasants who think in terms of group conflict are exceptional. Tensions remain focused on the conduct and personal characteristics of the landowner. As one peasant said: "No, I don't believe that all *patrones* think the same as he did. Not all the *patrones* are bad. The bad owners are very few."

It is in the historical background and the present situation on the *fundo* that we should seek the sociopolitical significance of the moment when the peasants suddenly emerge as protagonists of a collective action that breaks radically with the established institutional order. Our intent is to show to what extent this structural process corresponds to an effective change in peasant values and to the development of a group consciousness that extends beyond the particular situation in which it arises.

Preparation for the Takeover

Early in 1965 the peasants at Culiprán began to demand that the owner pay them the minimum wage established by law. Threatened by a strike, the owner signed an agreement in May, but it soon became evident that he had no intention of fulfilling the agreement. The peasants took their griev-ances to the *alcalde* (mayor) of Melipilla, who authorized a march as a means to pressure the owner into compliance with the contract. The peas-ants, however, rapidly became aware that the mayor was only demanding the legal minimum—the eight-hour day that was already supposed to be a national law. At the same time, the inspector of labor and the governor did not seem eager to give support to the peasant petitions. The landowner, for his part, began arbitrarily to impose a number of charges for the *regalías* that were traditionally part of the peasants' payment (pasturage for the peasants' livestock, the use of carts to transport firewood, and such). One *campesino* stated: ". . . the *patrón* took away all our *regalías*. He gave us an acre of land and rented us two acres. He took nine escudos from us for each animal, three escudos for a cartload of firewood, and we had to pay him 0.60 escudos for our bread."

It was in these circumstances that the peasants sought contact with the Socialist party through a peasant organizer who was already working on some of the neighboring *fundos*. With his help they elaborated and presented a much more complete petition, which they took to the provincial governor's office where a formal agreement (*acto de avenimiento*) was drawn up. When this too was ignored, the peasants took the initiative and organized a peaceful work stoppage of two days. The main point of the strike was to secure the approval of the petition requiring the owner to give one-half cuadra of land as a *regalía*. The possibility of expropriation was still not raised. When the strike also proved a failure, they called a meeting with the political organizers that was attended by some two hundred peasants. At this meeting, the organizers brought up the necessity of taking the *fundo* but asked that the decision be delayed until another meeting could be called.

The new meeting took place four days later and was more heavily attended. The peasants showed their intention of taking the *fundo*. Nevertheless, in spite of the general agreement about their decision, they were still afraid of losing their jobs. The president of the union assured them by saying that, if it was necessary for someone to die, he would be the first.

The agreement to take over the *fundo* was adopted at midnight in order to be ahead of the *carabineros*, who were being informed by some *empleados* or *inquilinos* who opposed the action. The administrator of the *fundo* had left, so that the only authority was that of the peasant leaders. An eyewitness of the events gave the following account of those dramatic moments:

> I happened to be on the hacienda Culiprán, staying at the home of my friend, a young worker of the *fundo*. He told me that that night there was to be a meeting to decide the future of the peasants whose petitions had been tied up in red tape for almost a year.
>
> We went to the soccer field where there was a game between the teams of the sports clubs of Culiprán and Molino San José. The home team won the game four to two.
>
> During the game I noticed an uneasiness in the people. They weren't concentrating on the game—there was emotion, nervousness, fear, and courage in every face. A number of tangled emotions were plain to any person who paid attention. And all these feelings became sharper when we heard the president of the union speak with modest words: *Compañeros*, we are meeting with all sincerity and seriousness, and mindful of the responsibility we are taking on, to decide what we will do about our problems that for so long have been without solution. The *patrón*

refuses to deal with us, the authorities turn their backs to us, the congressmen and the town council promised us much and have solved nothing for us. Only *compañero* M. has told us that we are right to ask for the *acto de avenimiento* to be carried out. We have discussed the problem before; now we must take the steps necessary to put an end to our needs and these delays. I turn the floor over to you."

Only one worker spoke after the president of the union: "It's not worth it to discuss the problems we have, since we all know them well enough. We know what we have to do. We know that the good will of the *patrón* and the authorities is never going to meet our demands. The only solution, as we have said several times, is to take the land now. Either they take care of our problem or they kill us all. The *carabineros* are already warned that we might take the *fundo* and they're arriving already. Taking over the *fundo* is the solution, and there is no other."

All this was carried on in soft voices. They voted on the motion to take the *fundo* and it was approved unanimously.

Right away a committee of delegates and directors was appointed to be in charge of the internal management of the conflict—leaving the leaders of the union for the job of dealing with the government authorities. Some *campesinos* were put in charge of closing the gates and all the *compañeros* were ordered to go to their houses and return right away with their tools and horses so that tactical measures could be taken, and for reasons of security that the mass of workers were not told about.

That night was one of fear and hope. In hushed voices people talked about the possibility of being pushed out violently by the police force in the early morning. No one slept, and they all stayed on foot in the intense cold with their tools ready for the defense. They had no fire, so that they wouldn't be identified and could defend themselves better. At dawn the trucks of the *carabineros* came, and a car driven by the administrator of the *fundo*. The *campesinos* formed a tight line of defense around the iron gate and part of the wire fence—they were prepared for action. But only the major of *carabineros* came near, and he addressed the *campesinos*:

"Which one of you is Segundo Núñez?"

"I am Segundo Núñez."

"Are you the owner of this *fundo*?"

"No, I am not the owner of the *fundo*. All of us are the owners of the *fundo*. Because we are united, we are all the owners of the *fundo*."

"Open these gates immediately and leave the area before I make you leave with my men."

"We do not open this gate to anyone—not to you or anyone."

"I have orders to get you out of here. The *fundo* doesn't belong to you, so get along or I'll make you leave in whatever way I have to. Do you think that I'm afraid of those weapons of yours?"

"And we're not afraid of your weapons either, I tell you." [They had gotten out with carbines in hand.]

"Open the gate, I tell you."

"Open it yourself, and if you come in with your head on your shoulders you'll leave without it if you even try to open this gate."

"Be careful with what you say . . . You'll see that I don't sell my hide cheaply and I'll take several of you with me."

"We will be shot and killed by you before we open this gate. We also know how to defend ourselves."

Then the major asked: "Tell me, what's wrong? Why did you take the *fundo*?"

"What's wrong with us is that we're fed up. They've been screwing us—the way they treat us. Now we're the owners of the land. We want the land for ourselves and we won't let it go. We'd rather die fighting now than die of hunger later because of that fop [*futre*]."

"So you want a fight. Do you really want to fight? Don't joke with me; answer if you want a fight, because if it's a fight you want we are here to give you the pleasure."

"No, we don't want to fight. We want the land. You've come here looking for a fight, but don't think that we're afraid. We aren't afraid to fight and we won't back down."

"It looks like you're all heated up, but I'm going to turn off that heat and leave you cold forever," said the Major.

"Yes, we're pretty hot all right, but you can't cool us off like you say, because we're going to fight until we take this *fundo* away from those who are starving us. We demand that they give us the land so we can work it. It seems that you want to fight, and we will fight to keep you from taking away what we have taken for ourselves."

Then the major said: "All right, all right, it's obvious that you're all excited, but the rain that's falling will cool you down. I like people like you. It's a pleasure to see fighting cocks. I suggest that you resolve this conflict in Melipilla, but first you have to return to your houses and get back to normal."

"Go back! Never. Not before our case is completely solved. The only thing they've done in Melipilla is delay us. It seems that the authorities are sold to the fop."

"Then I must be sold out, too," answered the major.

"That we don't know—you're the only one who knows about that."

"All right. We're leaving, but I'll come to pay you another visit later. Behave yourselves and be careful."

"Come whenever you want, come whenever you want—to talk or whatever. But don't think that you will put a foot inside the *fundo*. No one will pass."

This dialogue was the first confrontation between the rebels and the police, and it gave the *campesinos* more confidence in their movement. They discussed what each one had said to the *carabineros*, and their analyses of the events led them to the conviction that by standing up to the provocations of the police they had taken a positive step toward winning their cause. The *campesinos* agreed to continue their vigil and adopted different security measures prescribed by the political organizers, who had come from outside to stop the eviction. The defensive measures proposed by the organizers were perfected by the *campesinos* themselves. Soon other political leaders arrived, including some members of Parliament. They were informed of the encounter with the *carabineros* and of the major's threats. One of the organizers gave a speech offering to take the measures necessary (speak with the minister of the interior and the *intendant*) to avoid the interference of the police. This new offer of backing further reinforced the peasants' spirit.

The preceding description gives us a picture of the development of the conflict and its most characteristic elements. We may summarize this picture in the following points:

1. The arbitrary conduct of the landowner and the development of a negative but particularistic image of him. "The takeover happens when there is a bad *patrón*; if there is a good *patrón*, then there's no takeover."

2. The negligent behavior of the local authorities in collusion with the interests of the landowner, and the external support of persons perceived as "important" and "influential" in government. One of the peasants thought that "if they [the political organizers from Santiago] hadn't come, the people wouldn't have dared to take the *fundo*. They were the ones who gave us encouragement and all the plans." Others, speaking in the same vein, stated that "a man from Santiago was the one who organized the movement. We wouldn't have been able to do it alone." Another said, ". . . they [the peasants] had confidence because they were all united and because senators and deputies came from Santiago."

This discussion of outside influences gives rise to a series of questions. Without the participation of these outside elements, would the *campesinos* have been able to go so far? Would the conduct of the peasants have been the same? Did the peasants have other alternatives? The crux of the problem lies in determining whether these peasant "rebellions" are the expression of the emergence of the peasantry as a social class. The answer may lie in determining whether these collective actions that break with traditional patterns and paternalistic subjection are paralleled by the appearance and development of a group consciousness that outweighs the initiatives and distortions caused by the hacienda's institutional structure and value system. We intend to answer this question by analyzing different types of peasant consciousness according to the position occupied by the *campesino* on the *fundo*.

Peasant Consciousness

The Culiprán peasants overcame significant obstacles to seize the *fundo*. This objective fact spawns a number of consequences for the future evolution of the peasant group and the effects that similar action will have on other groups.

Is it possible that the first symptoms of class maturity are expressed in these movements, and that the stimulus thus provided for others to follow the same course contributes to the consolidation of a peasant class? According to any a priori scheme of "classes" the answer is affirmative because one begins with the supposition that class corresponds to the culmination of a long-term process involved with the contradictions inherent in the system. Those who do not accept the idea of class in the Marxist sense, but prefer to dissolve it into a thousand other concepts, do not recognize the appearance of a phenomenon that—class or no class—reflects new forms of social dynamism.

Without entering into a discussion of the sociological characteristics of the peasantry, let us establish the following hypothetical elements defining the class.

1. The complexity of the class due to the multifunctionality of the peasantry (its "polyvalence," to use the terminology of the Interamerican Committee for Agricultural Development's study of Brazil). The fact is that an enormous diversity of socioeconomic statuses is found within the class situation of the peasantry. The peasant performs diverse roles, and his position vis-à-vis the means of production therefore takes on different characteristics—forming a complex network of antagonistic interests.

2. The situation's internal heterogeneity means that the dynamics (actions and aspirations) of the peasants revolve around sectors that we call the "internal vanguard." These sectors may not be the same in all

the regions of a given country, and they also differ if compared over periods of time.

3. The local or national character of these internal sectors is important to our understanding of which contradictions actually mobilize the peasantry. The extent to which these may change because of different internal sectors has direct consequences for the development of peasant solidarity and an accurate conception of organization.

4. The scale or geographic extent of the peasant organization, in order to be efficient, must take observations 1 and 3 into account.

5. What we have established about the class situation of the peasantry should be understood together with the dimension of isolation that limits the peasant network of social relations and is characteristic of the hacienda's traditional system of tenancy. This aspect may lead the peasantry into a greater dependence upon its leadership—particularly its local leadership.

6. Finally, internal heterogeneity, isolation, and the greater necessity of local leadership determine that the peasantry's actions will take place on the level of mass movements—the action of different social strata in a single movement with its own contradictions rather than that of one homogeneous stratum on a national scale and influenced by similar contraditions.

Approach to the Analysis of Consciousness

With the objective of describing the elements that characterize the peasant consciousness as the peasants begin to participate in collective actions and the structure of the *fundo* is transformed, we have elaborated instruments that fulfill the functions of a typology. The typology has been worked up in light of the peasants' relation with the *patrón* and with the rest of the peasantry, for the nature of these relations reflects changes in the hacienda system—especially in its isolation from the exterior and in the functions of the system of mutual obligations and responsibilities.

In accordance with earlier criteria we can distinguish three types of consciousness that never occur in isolation but are interconnected. In spite of this overlapping, we may postulate their correspondence to three different stages in the evolution of consciousness: (1) paternalism, (2) trade-unionism, and (3) political consciousness.

1. Paternalistic consciousness can be broken down into the following characteristics:

a. The indispensability of the *patrón*. This concept should be approached from the point of view of the hacienda's economic functioning, and from that of the personal security of the peasant. Both aspects of indispensability reflect different degrees of subjection to the image of the *patrón* and, consequently, differences in the capacity and motivation to oppose him. As long as the peasant perceives the *patrón* as an indispensable element in the functioning of the estate, and identifies his own security with the system of mutual obligations and responsibilities, he will be an unconditional supporter of the *patrón*. On the other hand, if he sees the *patrón* as indispensable for the functioning of the estate but does not link him to his own security, or if he thinks that the existence of a boss other than the owner of the *fundo* is indispensable, then there are no obstacles to his emancipation from the owner. Nevertheless, it is necessary to remember that the different forms and degrees of subjection to paternalism depend upon the extent to which the *campesino*'s personal security is confused with his internal economic possibilities—in other words: the degree to which the system assures the peasant stability of status and possibilities of mobility.

    b. The perception of the owner as an isolated individual not identified with any social group is another of the characteristics of a consciousness subjected to paternalism. Its importance lies in the fact that it reflects the isolation that involves the peasant and his inability to think of himself in broader contexts. As will be seen, this idea permits the predominance of the particular situation defined by the peasant-owner relationship over the broader situation of an exploitative relation between *patrones* and peasants in general.

    c. A personal rather than group relation with the *patrón* is the third characteristic of this type of consciousness, and it is the result of the two preceeding characteristics. The peasant who sees the *patrón* as indispensable, who associates his own security with the owner in different ways and degrees, and who has developed no group consciousness necessarily bases his relations with the landowner in personal terms because they are the most functional for two persons cast in a very singular and isolated situation in which they are subject to reciprocal obligations and responsibilities.

    2. Trade union consciousness is a more advanced stage in which relations with the *patrón* can be undertaken by the group. This development introduces a further opening of the system, for the organized peasant enters into direct contact (or indirect contact through his leaders) with new realities that broaden the horizons of his knowledge and, to a lesser

extent, his system of social relations. The following elements are characteristic of this stage of consciousness.

a. Acceptance of the trade union type organization as a means of
achieving better conditions on the *fundo*. This organization is still subject
to the limits imposed by the *fundo*, but it represents the first indication
that the peasantry is transforming itself into an authority group.

b. The organized union's activity is limited to the *fundo* and does not
try to coordinate the peasants of other *fundos* as well. Though the *campesino* overcomes his internal isolation, he is still subject to the isolation of
the system, which supports the internal relations of dependency. He is no
longer an isolated individual; he is now part of an isolated group.

Organized action is limited to obtaining better wages and working conditions but stops short of attacking the *patrón* himself. The peasantry's
emerging authority group still has not become a competitive force, and the
peasant organization is satisfied to apply pressure while respecting the
existing authority structure. This is the critical point at which a complete
and rapid transformation of the peasant takes place. The intensification of
the pressure for demands may hasten the crisis of the system (with regard
to its capacity to satisfy those demands) and thereby accelerate the transformation of the peasantry from a simple authority group, still respectful
of traditional dependency relations, into an antagonistic authority group.
When this transformation takes place a third type of consciousness has
been achieved: political consciousness.

3. Political consciousness represents the maturation of the elements
contained in the trade union type of consciousness and the break with the
lingering traces of paternalistic subjection still found in the latter type (the
perception of the *patrón* as "necessary," for example).

But the movement from one type of consciousness to another is possible
only when external elements stimulate and support the transformation of
the peasant into a competitive authority group. Moreover, in order for the
change to come about, it is necessary for the hacienda system to be incapable of responding to the demands made upon it. If this condition is
not present it can be expected that the peasant movement will bog down
or begin to evolve in other directions, such as the acceptance of new forms
of work and remuneration while retaining respect for paternalistic authority.

In the political consciousness phase, the peasantry has become a group
with interests clearly contrary to those of the *patrón* whether or not he is
perceived as a good or a bad *patrón*. In this stage the peasant movement

expresses itself in two ways: First, a broader solidarity develops among the peasants, meaning that the specific context of group action is no longer the determining factor. The predominant view now reflects the more global context that defines the peasants as exploited regardless of their belonging to a specific system.

It must be noted, however, that the peasants, as an authority group, may carry out competitive actions without having reached this level of consciousness if the security derived from relying upon outside help takes the place of solidarity with the rest of the peasantry. In fact, the peasant's consciousness of the global context and his exploitation by the agricultural system is more often a result than a cause of the movement that seeks to remove the *patrón*.

The second direction that the *campesinos* may take in order to become an antagonistic group is the elimination of the *patrón* when this action comes to seem both necessary and possible. When these two dimensions of necessity and possibility are not integrated, the result is a series of intermediate forms of group consciousness on the part of the peasantry. From the point of view of this typology, we may say that until this integration takes place the group consciousness is inconsistent. It seems that the coincidence of "necessity" and "possibility" can take place once it is shown by concrete actions to be feasible. These actions are the result of demands made over a period of time on a system incapable of responding to them. The stimulus of external support aggravates the situation and permits the peasants to find themselves in real situations that make their strength obvious.

But just as these concrete experiences can contribute to pushing consciousness to a more global level, the opposite may also occur. Without the support of external factors, it is difficult for the peasant to develop a dynamic consciousness capable of sustaining itself. Also, it is possible to mistake apparently collective actions for the emergence of an antagonistic consciousness. Again, we feel that political consciousness is the product of these actions—not their cause.

The preceding concepts shape the analytical framework we have used to study peasant consciousness, its stages of development, and the consistency or inconsistency between its elements.

7. Analyses of Cases of Consciousness

The Leader

The peasant leader, who will be called N, took an active part in the takeover of the *fundo*, though at present he is not a member of the Comité Directivo del Asentamiento. He is fifty-five years old and was born on the *fundo*—"I was born and raised in this very house."

Until the takeover he worked as an *inquilino*. "I'm an *inquilino*; I've never done sharecropping—just a worker. . . . The rest are just plain *inquilinos*. *Obligados*, yes, sir. We don't have any *afuerinos* [migrant laborers] , either. The ones who came before could work here, but not anymore. It's been around ten years now that they haven't let *afuerinos* in; the real residents of the *fundo* work here—nearly all of them born and raised in Culiprán. The last contracts were made almost forty years ago. Almost all the *inquilinos* have lived here a long time."

N has had some political experiences in the past. He remembers, for example, that in 1920 there was a strike and a march on Melipilla that resulted in a raise in salary for his father. "That night—I was ten and shivering from the cold with my parents—we marched. We marched and we gained a little ground. In those days my father was making 80 cobres as an *inquilino* on the hacienda, but after the strike he made 1.20 pesos—they gave him a raise of 40 cobres."

"So I grew, and when I reached the age to do military service they also registered me to vote. When the election of the late Aguirre Cerda came along, the Peasant League was formed and I began to work as a leader. We were making 2.50 pesos by then, and they raised us to 3.20. When we got that raise the *patrón* axed a few of the *inquilinos* . . . They were fired for being mixed up in the Peasant League. That was when the Socialists joined us here."

He is not an isolated or uninformed person. "I have relatives: cousins and brothers and sisters here and in the neighboring *fundo* in San Miguel. Also in Santiago. My relatives are scattered in at least five different places. . . . I have lots of friends—on the *fundo* outside, and in Melipilla, too. It's a long way but sometimes we get to visit. Sometimes they come to see me, sometimes I go to see them."

Outside of his family, he sees friends who come to visit once a year. N says of his visits to the nearest town: "I don't go to Melipilla much, maybe three times a week now; but when there's a campaign and we have to put up posters we're there nearly every day."

His sources of information, however, are not limited to his personal relations. "The radio and newspapers tell me about what's going on outside . . ." His work brings him into town whenever it is necessary to sell his produce. "We eat what we need and sell the rest. . . . we take it to Santiago for the market because there is no market to speak of in Melipilla. We have to pay for freight costs. . . . Sometimes the cost is split up between several men, other times one man . . . pays the freight himself. We do that once a year and I go myself in one of the trucks we have here . . ." Thus, he sells his produce without any marketing facilities in the nearest town (Melipilla). Like all the *inquilinos,* he has a half cuadra of land and a few animals.

N thinks of himself as an important person. He says that he is well known because he has always been a fighter—citing his political past and his active participation in the takeover of the *fundo*. His political commitment to the Socialist party has influenced him, though his assimilation of this political doctrine is secondary in importance to his goals of becoming a small holder (*productor*) on the *fundo*. Nevertheless, N is able to appreciate political incentives and shows a certain capability in interpreting politics: ". . . five years ago . . . I read in a paper about Alessandri's agrarian reform. I called my *compañeros* together but they didn't believe me. . . . But I got them together and said: 'This is what's happening, *compañeros*, and this is what we are going to have to do.'

Later we met again, and I talked to them again, and finally some believed me."

Similarly, N's political personality is illustrated by his discussions with the *fundo* administrator. The informant shows himself to be very proud that the administrator considered him a political man. "The *patrón*, Don Ligualdo, knows me very well. One day when he was working here I came up and he greeted me before I reached him. 'What's up, Lafferte,' he said, because the administrator always called me Lafferte."

"Sometimes the son of the minister used to come here . . . and everyone stopped [work] when we started to talk politics. We started a conversation, and right away he wanted to talk politics with me. He got mad sometimes and started to chew me out, but I said: 'Don't get mad. We're just talking. Why get excited if it's just talk?' He would leave laughing. 'Just as long as you remember I'm boss,' he'd say, but when we got to talking again, he'd get mad again. 'Don't get so upset, Don Luis,' I said, 'Now we have to beat you—once and for all we will have to win.'"

The informant imagines that the others consider him one of their leaders because he is alert and well informed. In reality, however, he is neither one of the most influential leaders nor one of the most prestigious persons in the movement. He is a peasant who combines his rebellious and nonconformist behavior with a strong profit motive. The aspirations he has for his sons are illustrative of his orientation. "I'd also like for my sons to be farmers and make some money, because you always know that agriculture is going to go up . . ." N's great hope for the future is that his income will reach five thousand escudos. All his attitudes are influenced by the example of a relative who has risen economically in the town. As he says: "What I have always wanted is to make money and have a better life. To own a little bit of land where I am boss—some money and eight cuadras to work with my sons. I already have an opportunity because I have a friend who says that I don't have to kick in with anything and he'll open an account for me in the bank. Then, he says: 'If you need livestock I'll buy them and we'll fatten them on your land and then I'll sell them for you.' . . . He's a businessman who lives in Melipilla . . ."

N's entrepreneurial tendencies, his preference for private property, and his confidence in his economic success explain his attitudes toward other things. He thinks that after a two-year period of joint ownership the land will be divided. Nevertheless, he is not against the cooperative working of the *fundo*, because "if we don't get along well we won't divide anything." The informant's acceptance of work "in community" is not of great

importance, because he has no confidence in it. It is really only a concession made to his ideological commitments. N projects his personal pref-
erences to the other *campesinos*: "I think our people want the division
because each one wants his own little plot. I'm for dividing it up."

The informant's aspiration to own a piece of land (eight cuadras) that
some rich relatives have told him he can work with his sons and make
three thousand escudos per cuadra, is complemented by the idea that a
new *patrón* would be unacceptable: "... it's better to be working on your
own land than on somebody else's." On the other hand, he sees no possibility of having a good *patrón*, because "I think that almost all the
patrones are like this Marín [owner of Culiprán]. The first one that fell
was this one they kicked out, Catán.[1] Catán and Marín are the same."

His refusal to submit to a new *patrón* does not constitute a rejection of
all forms of leadership. He believes that some form of external and internal
leadership would be best, because there has to be someone to tell the
peasants what and when to plant. The traditional image of the *patrón*,
with his avarice, arbitrariness, and bad management of the *fundo*, is to be
substituted by the small landholder capable of making progress with the
help of his own family. This new form of landowner, however, needs the
direction of a *jefe* to guide and help him, and in whom he can have
confidence. "I think there have to be *jefes*; there is even a *jefe* here....
That is how it always has to be.... there has to be a *jefe*. Here, I think
that there always ought to be a man in charge of the farmers.... He goes
to each plot and says, 'You have to plant potatoes here, do this there,
plant that here.' He tells them what they should plant."

It is clear, then, that in becoming a landowner the informant does not
reject all idea of dependency. Certainly the new relationship does not
include the elements of paternalism and authority found in the relation
with the *patrón*, but it does reflect the insecurity of the peasant—an insecurity that must be taken into account in order to understand the
dynamism that may be expected from the peasantry. This period of insecurity can be a propitious time for the imposing of certain forms of
organization and orientation on the peasants. The long period of consolidation makes the peasant malleable because he is free to test social for-
mulas against his own experience. This pragmatic approach is basic to the
dynamics of the peasantry. Perhaps it is what G. Gurvitch was thinking of

---

[1] A landowner whose property was expropriated because of his mistreatment of the
peasants and because of the abandoned nature of his land.

when he said that in the peasantry, as in the bourgeoisie, economic interests take precedence over those of class. In other words, the peasant does not change himself merely because of the change of the tenancy system. The peasantry cannot be considered a definite, mature, and stable social sector, since the peasant affirms himself as part of such a sector only in the course of the polarizing process. For this reason, the social and economic effects of the modification of the system cannot be considered by themselves; the changes provoked in the peasantry as a class must also be studied. The peasantry's heterogeneity carries with it many contradictions that may develop when influenced by the change in tenure—spawning new orientations or accentuating latent contradictions that will affect the behavior of the peasants. The first anomaly presented by the study of agrarian reform, then, is the peasantry itself; for it is often assumed that the reform affects it as a class, when many times the reform only polarizes internal tensions and stimulates the process of the consolidation of the class.

The necessities of the peasants, once they have taken the land again, show the dependency on external factors. Aside from the farm implements and the desire to have a cooperative "to bring us goods: canvas, plows, rope, bolts, and everything we'd need for a cooperative," N thinks that the assistance of a politician is needed more than that of an agronomist: "We don't really need an agronomist because we . . . well, just look at me, I'm sure that I could put him in the shade."

The politician symbolizes external support without which the takeover would not have been possible: "the plans have to be well made, because, listen—if the plan is badly made, I think we could be killed. If we hadn't gone to Santiago to study the plan three days before, then it wouldn't have worked."

This perception of the politician as the most important element is not surprising, for it grows out of the peasant's insecurity about his political status. His own experiences are something that he knows and dominates and that will not lead him into unfamiliar situations he may find impossible to manage. On the other hand, the possession of land gives the peasant a status with which it is difficult to cope, because the change in status does not cause the immediate internalization of the rights and obligations inherent in that status. It is for this reason that the peasant appreciates the necessity of help and guidance during the period of adaptation to his new role. Naturally, the character of this aid is political rather than technical, since the power factors that made the new role possible are themselves political. As long as the peasant has not completely adapted to the demands of his new status, the aid of these external factors is required.

External political aid has two main functions: (1) It aids in the structuring of new patterns of behavior, for it is possible for a maladjustment to arise between the traditional patterns of agricultural work and the need for new patterns to be instituted because of the institutional change that has taken place. (2) It legitimizes the new status or, rather, supports the legitimacy of the change. The new situation achieved by the peasants depends largely on external supports because it has not been the exclusive result of a spontaneous action (movement). This stage can be critical if the appropriate external aid is not present to provide elements of legitimation in the situation of the peasant class.

The leader interviewed is aware that the peasantry must constitute an authority group and rid itself of the *patrón*—an awareness not restricted to Culiprán alone, but which is extended to the peasantry as a whole. Nonetheless, the peasants of Culiprán feel that their position of leadership is limited in the case of good *patrones*. N says, "... I can tell you that something big is going to happen here—something very big. They are all watching us because the people of Culiprán are going to own the land. If I went to the neighboring *fundo* here and explained that to them, they'd come right over. . . . The other *campesinos*, from what my friends and relatives around here tell me, are very preoccupied with what we've done. They're already beginning to do the same things we did. They are holding meetings, and even the *campesinos* of the San Manuel *fundo*, where there is a very good *patrón*, are already having meetings. I don't want to get involved in that, because their *patrón* was good to us during the takeover."

For N, the peasantry is an authority group that must put pressure on the *patrón* through its organization—going so far as to call strikes if its demands are not met. N believes that this is true on all the *fundos* where the peasants could achieve this organization with a little stimulus: "They have to be brave if they're going to [take over the *fundo*], because there are many who aren't going to think the way we do." The informant has visited other *fundos* to teach the peasantry how to organize a strike and to show them that the only solution to their problems is to take the land.

The idea of the authority group is emphasized to the point that the peasants are turned into pressure groups when they begin to perceive agrarian reform as a response to the de facto situation they themselves have created. Their feeling is that agrarian reform will only be instituted under pressure. The pressure itself, however, carries with it contradictions that may make it vary in intensity or direction. "I can't believe that the president is going to say to the *campesinos*, 'I'm going to give you an agrarian reform here.' You have to take the *fundo* for that. And even if the owners organize against us . . . the people will always fight them."

In summary, we may say that the leader (N) has few of the characteristics of the paternalistic consciousness phase of our typology. He does not consider the *patrón* as an isolated individual but identifies him with his group. At the same time, he does project some of the personal characteristics of the *patrón* of Culiprán on the rest of the landowners, and this keeps him from acting against a *patrón* who is perceived as "good." In any case, N is aware of an opposition of interests, rejects a private or personal relationship with the *patrón*, and therefore does not believe that the *patrón* is indispensable. ". . . if they [the owners] disappear the people will be much better off, because the owners will have to go to the city. They'll go to the towns, and on the *fundos* the people who made them rich will be working for themselves. The money that the rich men made is going to be for the worker. I don't think anyone will be poor—only the lazy ones."

In spite of this belief in the owner's dispensability, N feels that he should be replaced by some other form of leadership to provide a measure of security in the decision-making process. In this case it seems that the image of the *patrón* has lost its paternalistic content while retaining a certain functionality that may be transfered to another directing agent seen as indispensable to the organization of work. The *patrón* disappears but his place is taken by the leadership of a new element (preferably political) that fills a need characteristic of the stage of insecurity mentioned earlier. While it is true that there is a clear agreement that *patrones* are not indispensable, the idea of elimination is not necessarily extended to all *patrones*—especially not to those who satisfy the aspirations of the peasants.

"All the peasants are in the fight together," though they are divided between those who oppose the *patrón* and those who support him. This notion, though it cannot be affirmed that it has any class content, at least approaches the stage of *toma de consciencia* (becoming politically conscious) and defines different degrees of solidarity found within the peasantry because of their different levels of dependence on the *patrón*. The elimination of the *patrón* is possible, but not always necessary, and the desire for his elimination is a general attitude that does not necessarily have to be translated into reality. From this point of view, the peasants' struggle is not irreconcilable with the status of the *patrón*, and when the *fundo* is taken over it is as a consequence of the negligent, petty, and arbitrary behavior of the landowner. In this sense, the system can tolerate concrete union activity combined with certain social reformism.

The takeover itself is a radical way of obtaining improved living and working conditions. The critical factor that decides the step from the unionization stage (still respectful of the dominant status relationships on the *fundo*) to the takeover, with all its changes in tenure and authority relations, lies in the *patrón's* desire and ability to satisfy the economic demands made by the peasants. N thinks that this form of action (the takeover) can be utilized by the rest of the peasantry; but fundamentally, his own attitude toward the takeover grows out of the perceptions he has of himself as a leader and political militant.

From the preceding we may gather that, for N, the peasants can be transformed into a pressure group by the intransigence of the *patrón* and the realization that he enjoys the complicity of the local authorities. But N is not led to think that there is such a thing as peasant solidarity: "Each one has to work things out himself." His vision is restricted to the events on Culiprán, which were little affected by group consciousness, and he does not know what allies the peasants can count on. In spite of his political "affiliation," his perception of the happenings is still limited to a "reformist" type of action that has no ideological content and emphasizes peasant pragmatism. He therefore feels it is necessary that the "allies" of the peasantry be ministers of state and congressmen—of any party—who can be useful as elements of external support. The support of a deputy or senator is seen as more valuable than a broad and coordinated action by all the peasants because the politicians can deal directly with ministers or the president of the Republic—applying pressure through the regime's official channels. The informant emphasizes the possibility of a broad and coordinated action only as a reaffirmation of his own importance as an activist. In the interview he repeats that without the support of the congressmen and outside activists "I don't think the people would have had the courage to take the land. They [congressmen] were the ones who came to give us encouragement and make all the plans. . . . some of the people were afraid. There were some whose knees were knocking . . ."

The description of N is full of the contradictions appropriate to a peasant who still exists in a stabilized situation. Because he is in the midst of a process of maturation, his definitive evolution is in a certain sense susceptible to politico-ideological manipulations, which, in order to be effective, must begin by recognizing his peasant pragmatism. Failure to take this pragmatism into consideration could produce very unpleasant surprises, especially since his case is found within a context of change like the agrarian reform.

In spite of what has been said about the contradictions and lack of structure in the peasant situation, a few characteristics are clear in the case of N. The elements that characterize his consciousness are as follows: (1) the *patrón* is dispensable, but his elimination is not a necessity; (2) the *patrón* is identified with a social group, but this group is identified as a projection of the personal characteristics of the owner of Culiprán; and (3) the relationship with the owner is a group relation rather than a personal or private one. These three characteristics demonstrate that the informant does not have a traditional paternalistic type of consciousness, though some traces still remain. This remnant is clearly seen in his attitude toward "the necessity to eliminate the *patrón*" and the way in which he identifies the *patrón* group by projecting the image of his former *patrón*. If an owner does not conform to this image, there is no conflict of interests for N.

Furthermore (4) the informant agrees with unionization of the workers as long as these organizations guarantee their success by seeking external support and by not limiting themselves only to the internal mobilization of the *fundo*; (5) the peasant's struggle is restricted to these objectives but it lacks an understanding of the external world defined in terms of class; and (6) for N, the attack on the status of the *patrón* is only the culmination of a previous process of negotiations for better conditions. These three characteristics show that the informant possesses elements of the trade union and political stage of consciousness. Although he is no longer identified with the traditional form of paternalism, he is still subject to his notions regarding the type of leadership most able to give him the security of organization and planning. The same phenomenon is observed in his preference for a group rather than private relationship with the owner of the *fundo*.

In spite of the internalization of values regarding the dispensability of the *patrón* and the rejection of a personal and particularistic relationship with him, however, the idea that success is possible without necessarily coming into conflict with the *patrón* from the outset suggests that the political components do not weigh as heavily for N as the remaining traces of paternalism.

Our picture of N, then, is one of a consciousness in the process of breaking away from its traditional paternalistic elements and moving toward true politization. It is, in other words, a consciousness evolving toward integration of the different elements we have analyzed. The process can be summarized thusly: the concept of the *patrón's* dispensability must be completed by the idea of the necessity of his elimination; the decision to take over the land must not be limited to the success achieved during the trade union stage; and, finally, the search for external support should be oriented by the significance that the takeover has in the context of opposition of interests. In short, the change must be made at the level of power relations rather than simply in status relations within the prevailing agrarian structure. It is in light of this concept of power relations that N evaluates the support received by the peasantry: emphasizing the ability of supporting elements (congressmen, ministers) to use the decision-making channels of the institutional structure, rather than counting upon the masses' potential for pressure.

N has not evolved to the stage of political consciousness, even though some ingredients of this third type of consciousness are present. Objectively, for example, N perceives an opposition of interests, but for him this opposition is conditioned by his entrepreneurial attitudes—his desire to become a small landowner. It is in this context that he differentiates between the *apatronados* and the *no apatronados*. The *apatronados* (*empleados*, for example), are those whose aspirations have been satisfied on the *fundo* because of certain privileges extended by the *patrón*, or those who have not developed an awareness of their own interests and therefore lack any incentive to break their relations of dependence.

The first stirrings of class consciousness revolve around the status of a small holder (*productor*) on the hacienda. Consciousness develops at the same rate as the certainty of taking the land and the militant peasant's ever sharper awareness of the differences between himself and others who oppose the change because they have already enjoyed good working conditions for many years.

Because this embryonic consciousness arises from the experience acquired in the takeover of the *fundo*, it only reflects the inequalities between *inquilinos* and *empleados*. It does not extend to the situation of the rest of the peasantry or to the other types of labor present on the *fundo* (*afuerinos* and *voluntarios*). N's perspective is local, but he is able to generalize about the process where similar conflicts are involved. The unknown factor is the evolution that this early consciousness of interests will undergo as the frustrated status of *productor* is progressively modified by the change of the system of tenancy, and the peasant's expectations finally begin to coincide with reality.

This new dynamic is the basis for stating that the first conflict will not be the only one, for once the change of the traditional structure begins, the peasantry begins to polarize as a class.

During the internal conflict within the hacienda system, one factor remains constant and seems to be typical of the consciousness that rejects paternalism because of the growing polarization. The *patrón* is not seen as indispensable, and his elimination comes to be an acceptable possibility— though it is not felt that it will always be necessary. A real change of consciousness is reached when the elements of "necessity" and "possibility" begin to merge. Theoretically, the maturation of a class consciousness will take place when this fusion is complete.

For the moment we will limit ourselves to the formulation of some hypotheses.

If the conflict in the trade union stage is marked by the presence of external elements, the level of the struggle may be elevated. But if the movement is oriented toward institutional channels, it will become more difficult for the *campesino* to convince himself of the necessity of eliminating the *patrón*. The consequence will be the transformation of the peasantry into a pressure group, and not a competitive authority group demanding the elimination of the owner. This tendency is accentuated when the peasantry forms bureaucratic organizations that depend financially on functional relations with the institutional structure. Such dependence imposes a passive attitude upon the peasants because their raw power of pressure is replaced by the efficiency of the organization (union) that represents them. None of these factors will stimulate the maturation of the peasantry as a class (active solidarity among peasants) or lead to development of an awareness of belonging to a larger system in which other exploited groups face similar conflicts with the patronal authority.

At this point it is necessary to clarify the concept of antagonism as it applies to the particular situation. In truth, when we refer to the conflict of peasants with owners, we are speaking of a complex network of conflicts derived from the multiple roles the peasant may play. The conflict can take on different meanings and therefore orient the peasant in different directions, depending on the structure of internal roles and the importance of these for the totality of the peasants' activities. For example, if the predominant role is that of a frustrated small holder or market farmer within the hacienda system, the tendency will be to establish this type of economy after the takeover. On the other hand, if the dominant peasant role is that of simple salaried worker, the conflict can give rise to a different kind of economic system that may even allow the reorganization of the old patronal economy on other foundations.

The maturation of the peasant consciousness, according to the type of conflict that underlies it, will vary in both speed and substance. Thus, in the case of N, consciousness has developed in the context of a conflict between economies (patronal and *inquilino*) largely because the *fundo* is in a process of decomposition. But the economic conflict, as it deepens, also begins to take on political aspects and contributes to the political radicalization of the informant: "... if the *patrón* still doesn't give in [to the petition], we'll take the land." The radicalization of N is the direct consequence of patronal intransigence and the owner's alliance with the local authorities, coupled with N's own certainty of external aid. The entire process, however, is dominated by the meaning that the conflict has for N—to make him a medium-sized landowner. In effect, his radicalization consists of denying the need for the landowners while setting himself up to replace them. It is a political radicalization that drives N into a direct conflict with the owner and the authority that supports him, but it takes place within the framework of a mentality that is clearly conservative and ownership oriented.

The possibility of N's radicalized consciousness growing into one of global solidarity with the different peasant groups is hindered by the nature of the conflict that motivates him. The desire to become a landowner defines the extent of the conflict for N and is therefore the measure of the maturation of his consciousness. The definition of this consciousness is limited by the frame of reference within which he can achieve his aspirations—the *fundo*. Therefore, to the extent that the major conflict is of this nature, the tendency of the peasants toward isolation will intensify. A *campesino* who transforms his *regalías* into the basis of a small or medium landholding does not need the support of peasants outside his particular system. On the contrary, he may develop attitudes of social differentiation toward them, and solidarity of interests may even develop exclusively among those who have achieved some improvement of their conditions.

In this way, isolation is accentuated within the new structure of tenancy, and this traditional social isolation can cause the stagnation of the development of a new and broad consciousness. Later developments will depend upon the appearance of new conflicts, but at this point it is quite possible that the peasant class, as we understand it, will break up—originating a series of new internal conflicts.

What new antagonisms will arise for N? How will his change in status influence the development of his consciousness? How will he be affected by the discrepancies between entrepreneurial aspirations and the possibility of satisfying them? At present he is affirming his status as a small farmer, but undoubtedly this will not be his definitive position. How this final position will emerge from his own transformation during and after the agrarian reform is an open question for all peasant groups.

We should not forget the new forces that will develop because of the experience that permitted N to open many new alternatives to himself by overcoming the obstacle represented by the hacienda system. Once in motion, the peasantry may go beyond the agrarian reform itself.

The Dissident Employee (Empleado)

D is sixty years old; he was born on the *fundo* and has worked there all his life. His job was that of foreman (*campero*) in charge of livestock. The owner gave him as a *regalía* one cuadra of choice land, which allowed him to sell a part of his produce in the capital. "A year ago this month I sold two truckloads of potatoes in Santiago. I paid one thousand pesos a sack for freight and sold two hundred sacks in February." This commercial activity has permitted him to establish links with the outside that go beyond his visits to Melipilla, "to buy what we need. We always buy wholesale there, but you also have to buy things from the salesmen who come out here if you need something in a hurry."

D shows himself to be a person concerned about keeping informed. "I listen to the news on the radio every morning, at one o'clock, and every night. I know about everything that's going on in the country and in Europe." He is sure of himself and has planned for the future. He was one of a group of workers favored by the owner; after the takeover these employees more often tend to have an ambivalent attitude toward the new situation than one of open opposition.

D's attitudes are at once influenced by nostalgia for the order of things upset by the takeover and by the realistic spirit that keeps him from marginalizing himself in relation to the new possibilities offered by the *asentamiento*. His is the conflict of a man who finds himself in an ambiguous situation caused partly by the very entrepreneurial ability, self-confidence, and sense of foresight that made him prosperous.

D's mentality and attitudes are largely determined by the fact that the takeover means the end of a situation favorable to him: the status that he enjoyed because of the personal relationship with the landowner, with whom all D's possibilities for economic improvement rested. In other words, he was able to capitalize on his "subjection to the *patrón*." It is not surprising, then, that his defense of the traditional structure should be couched in terms of the necessity of the *patrón* to manage the hacienda and assure the personal security of the *inquilino*. His privileged situation leads him to take an individualistic attitude appropriate for a man who has been able to handle himself to his best advantage, conforming to the system by identifying his own possibilities for personal progress with the security extended to him by the *patrón*. Consequently, as long as it is possible for him to retain his advantages, his criticism of the new situation is determined by his status as a successful man who values the ability and will to work and takes advantage of the opportunities that present themselves. Hence, for D, those who have promoted and approved of the takeover of the *fundo* are the failures who want to receive everything on a silver platter.

D sees the movement to take over the *fundo* as more than a simple economic demand. In his opinion it constitutes a whole new way of thinking that he does not accept and that disturbs him. He longs for the traditional values personified by the hardworking and prudent man: one who is able to take advantage of the chances the hacienda offers to the opportunistic peasant. In spite of his negative opinion of the takeover itself and those who led it, it is this very attitude that leads him to want to take advantage of the possibilities offered by the new situation. In this he reaffirms the incentive that always directed his opportunism in the past: his status as an independent farmer.

D believes that the *fundo* requires an authority able to assure a hierarchical organization. The expulsion of the landowner creates internal chaos in which the peasants, although they know their work, cannot function properly. The hacienda cannot continue without the owner: "It's not that they don't know how to do the work here. They know the land and the work and what should be planted, but what I'm saying is that, if they take that *fundo* from the owner, there will probably be difficulties—like not respecting their leaders."

Authority must be respected in order for there to be organization. Therefore, when the *patrón* whom D respected disappears, so does all authority. Obedience no longer exists, "because now the people have rebelled ... There is another way to live now." And in the wake of this break with patronal authority, "my opinion is that one doesn't live as well as before. I think that the people have lost their respect. . . . In some things you can't help but notice that they've lost respect. In one thing: in this 'modern' way of living—where everything has to change, and the political ideas, too."

The vacuum created by the absence of the landowner and the authority derived from his personal prestige is filled by leaders recruited from among the population of the *fundo*. In this thinking the informant shows a fairly closed concept of the "group," which tends to create its own values of legitimacy: "People from here—from the *fundo*—would have to be in charge because outsiders don't know our problems. They'd have to be from here even if they didn't have the prestige of the *patrón*."

The new and irreversible situation becomes all the more complex for D because it involves changes in values, and the necessity of adaptation to new circumstances. Nevertheless, he remains outside the movement and continues to act and think in accordance with his own values, such as his perception of the *patrón*.

An indication of his tendency toward adaptation, however, is his desire that the new leaders be recruited from among the peasants of the *fundo*. Similarly, this preference may reflect the group's isolation and the peasant's feeling of belonging to a group that has succeeded in setting itself apart from the other peasants. Most significantly, however, it illustrates the fact that for D the *patrón* was more important as a means to achieving his own ends than as a symbol of authority and prestige. After the take-over, the informant's pragmatism leads him to prefer a leader who knows the *fundo* rather than someone who simply imposes authority.

In spite of his tendency to adapt, D maintains his marginality in many ways, the result being an imbalance between his pragmatism and his devotion to other value structures. The imbalance is reflected in his insistence that the security a good *patrón* can provide is preferable to independent farming. It is not surprising that even in this idea he contradicts himself by showing desire to work a piece of land independently. "Work in the country is more secure, and it's better to have security—even if you have to obey orders—than to be more free, as you say, in the city."

D's dependence upon and his loyalty to the *patrón* should be understood as functional necessities for him. Clearly, this is a case of what we will call "instrumental paternalism." Through the system of "give and take" he has achieved a privileged position within the hacienda. His pragmatism impels him to take advantage of the structure of paternalistic authority through different types of opportunism and accommodations that identify him subjectively with the *patrón*: "All my life I have voted for the Conservatives. All my life I have been a Christian—since I came of age . . . Yes, sir, all my life with the Conservatives, because I saw that, if one doesn't live with the people who have money, well, who are you going to live with? . . . You ask me why? Because it's the most orderly and peaceful way to live. You get along better with the *patrones* who like you. So the future is easier for you . . ."

There are several important points to be made about this pragmatism. First, one may think that this kind of political opportunism would demand that the *campesino* have a very clear idea of the nature of his antagonism with the landowner. If such an awareness is not present—as in the case of D—it is not surprising that some of the peasant's behavioral standards are influenced by the *patrón*, and that he tries to achieve his objectives by allying with or taking advantage of one who has already achieved success. D sees the *patrón* as a model, and he feels no antagonism toward him, because he has been able to progress due to the *patrón's* help. If the security D needs is defined by the *patrón*, why should he not win the good will of the *patrón* as reinforcement for his effort to better himself? The informant's identification with the *patrón* is based upon this functional management of the dependent relationship; as long as this relationship remains possible without conflicts, it will be D's model.

Nevertheless, the conflict becomes ever more difficult to avoid as the system of cash payment (instead of the *regalía*) becomes necessary and generalized. The traditional *regalía* system, however, can be preserved for a few loyal *inquilinos* even as it is taken away from the rest of the *fundo* population. This loyal nucleus of favored *inquilinos* has an attitude toward the *patrón* that is conditioned by the old system of "exchange of services." D shows this mentality in his description of his family's history: "We were all born in this house. My grandfather built it and he died when he was ninety-five years old. So we've had this house for more than one hundred years, and do you know why? Because we've gotten along well with the people who have owned the *fundo*. The *patrones* before gave us land. They thought well of my grandfather, and of my father after him. So we've always led an honorable, good life."

This relationship is the standard by which D evaluates the change that has taken place on the *fundo*. Since the *patrón* has ceased to be instrumental in D's objectives, D is no longer tied to the past in a way that keeps him from seeking his best advantage in the new situation. This attitude is clear in D's concept of loyalty: "As for me, the *patrón* was always very good to me because we were brought up together. He's always given me all my food, and everything I have I owe to him. Why should I say anything bad about him?"

D's defense of his image of the *patrón* is made on the grounds of pragmatism. In it, he reveals the most important aspect of the *patrón's* arbitrariness—the discrimination that leads peasants who are not in favor to rebel. "Did the *patrón* have any defects? I didn't think he had any. He was a man of the law—except for a few little things—to those he liked—to those he didn't like, no."

As a successful man, however, D sees this discrimination as justified. "Even if there are others who don't have as much—who haven't risen as high—because you know that everyone has his place on the ladder. Not everyone can be the same on a *fundo*. There are privates, corporals, a sergeant, and then the colonels and so forth." Moreover, this attitude leads him to interpret the poor conditions of the rest of the *inquilinos* as the result of their inability to take advantage of their opportunities. "Of course, not everyone can live just the same, because we're not all equal, right? If there are so many other people of my age, why haven't they risen on the scale, too? I believe it's because they have a different way of thinking [*moral de pensar*]. They don't have to be loafers or gamblers or drunks. They have had the same opportunities I have but they haven't been able to be more than I am. If I've got some savings it's because I've been more economical. And I had kids who were better adjusted to the things of life."

The criterion D uses to justify these internal differences is raised to the level of a "natural necessity" that precisely reflects the mentality of the highest stratum of society—the landowners. There is similarity in the way that privileges are legitimized, however much they differ in magnitude and significance.

In this situation, D's preference for private, personal relations with the *patrón* is evident. He rejects all forms of collective action or union organization: ". . . I'm not for the unions. Don't even mention them to me [laughs]. I can't even stand to think about them. A union, at my age? What do I need an agrarian union for—now that the *patrón* is gone? . . . I didn't even want a union when we had a *patrón*, because he and I got along. How could I go against my *patrón* when I was on good terms with him and he gave me all the privileges: pasture for the animals, and milk cows. How could I go against him?"

D shows a profound individualism, which, together with his political opportunism, is an aspect of the pragmatism with which he has acted. What is clear is that, by rejecting the takeover because it is of no benefit to him, he does not place himself in opposition to the other *inquilinos*. "I'm not saying that the others don't have the right to form a union. I'm not unreasonable. If they didn't get along with the *patrón*, then I can almost say that they have a right."

But he excludes himself. He remains marginal and even refuses to allow his sons to take part in any action or organization linked to the takeover of the *fundo*. He defends himself by saying that things were better before the ouster of the landowner because then he had both land and security. "[Now] they can't get their personal documents brought up to date. Family men have gone without their documents and the hospitals won't take them. . . . I heard one man who was complaining a lot because they wouldn't fix his papers. They have to be in order so that the family allowance can be paid. The *patrón* used to take care of that, but if everyone is *patrón*, what with the *asentamiento*, will it be the same?"

He re-emphasizes the dimension of security when he declares that "It's better to have one *patrón*—as long as he's a good one." This preoccupation is due to the fact that D had achieved his economic objectives while the *patrón* was still on the *fundo*. He was satisfied and could rely on the *patrón's* support in his old age. After the takeover, however, his fear of having to compete with younger men in work he feels incapable of performing competitively may determine his reticence. This attitude is common in older men who resist incorporation into communal work and even are reluctant to accept a piece of land of their own. The reticence, on the other hand, may well be created by others who are loath to share the work with those who lack the physical conditions necessary. Tensions among the peasants due to their greater or lesser dedication to their work are of great importance if we wish to establish modes of cooperative work in the community. D believes, for example, "at my age I can't work alongside young men." The appropriate response to this insecurity is to resolve the problem in the same way that older *inquilinos* did before the takeover: "What I'll do is I'll put my son to work . . ."

The key to D's behavior, then, is found in the privileged conditions he enjoyed on the hacienda before the takeover. These enable him to say that the rebellion was made by failures and malcontents—those who lacked the foresight to save and to organize their family lives. This attitude is confirmed, and D's pragmatism is reasserted by his conviction that his own entrepreneurial ability will once again allow him to make a place for himself in the new situation. The same spirit of accommodation that allowed him to achieve satisfactory conditions on the hacienda supports his belief that he is more capable and will again rise faster than the others. "If I've got the means to work with, how are they going to make as much as I do?" Of course, he wants to work independently, "because when everyone works together you're never going to make money." His desire to take advantage of the new circumstances ("just give me three cuadras and I'll start to work them tomorrow") leads him to re-evaluate his relations with the *patrón*.

At the same time that the new situation stimulates his entrepreneurial abilities, it broadens his range of demands—many of which were difficult to achieve when the *patrón* still managed the hacienda. "I would have asked the *patrón* to give us more benefits: pieces of land to farm, and help when we needed it—money or whatever—in case someone ran out of capital to work with and needed a loan, because that would increase production. Yes, I believe that now that can be done. Before, with the *patrón*, I don't know." As long as the *patrón* was the means to satisfy his aspirations for land, D supported him; but when new possibilities are opened for the informant, he does not hesitate to break away from the *patrón*'s tutelage.

From this point of view, D's case tends to be similar to that of N, because their driving motivations are similar. Each tends to be oriented by "territorial" motivations, and the differences between them are determined by the level of progress they have reached within the *fundo*. N was the victim of the *patrón*'s arbitrariness, while D was one of the favored few. Their differences in status determine the differences in their attitudes toward the takeover, though these discrepancies will not necessarily persist once the new situation becomes stabilized.

After the takeover it is theoretically possible that a conflict may arise between these two types of *campesino* due to their differing ideas about the definitive system of tenure. N might opt for communal ownership of property, while the *empleado* (D) would tend to prefer family ownership. During the period of insecurity between the takeover and the final decision about the tenure system it is possible to direct the peasant toward one or the other solution; but the primary factor will be the realism of the peasant who will decide the form of tenure according to his own concrete experience. This is as true for the "politicized" peasants like N as it is for those who, in the new circumstances, continue to maintain the positions they upheld before the takeover, though without the limitations the hacienda system imposed. In this light it is interesting to examine the relations and mutual influences between the two types of peasant.

In attempting to sum up the most relevant characteristics of D's consciousness, we can say that he retains the dimension of indispensability of the *patrón* in two aspects: indispensability for the functioning of the estate, and indispensability for D's personal security. Basically, both of these aspects are the same, and they determine the rest of the characteristics exhibited by D. The *patrón* is an element of support for D's personal progress, while the *fundo* itself is the circumstantial setting in which the relation with the *patrón* takes place. The importance of the *patrón* to the functioning of the *fundo* then, is measured by the owner's ability to guarantee the stability D needs in order to achieve his objectives. In such a relationship, when the *patrón* disappears, D quite easily substitutes independent work in his place, because he immediately wants to take advantage of the new possibilities opened to him, although he himself would never be able to initiate an action against the *patrón*.

D is oriented by a more-or-less rational mentality. He does not limit himself to the concept of the *fundo*, nor does he identify subjectively with either the *fundo* or the *patrón*. The hacienda is only the setting against which his ordered and planned conduct based upon his personal relation with the landowner can be used to gather savings and attain a position of relatively individual success.

Because his status is the result of a relation of mutual confidence between him and the *patrón*, D's relationship with the *patrón* is defined in individual rather than group-oriented terms. In this sense it seems clear that D is an integral element of the very structure of patronal power, for he is a unit of support recruited and bound to the *patrón* through the system of exchange of services and favors. This system not only functions for the good of the *patrón* by cementing his influence through a loyal nucleus of workers, but it also works in the interest of the peasant who comes to be an element of support for the system rather than simply a subject of it. Driven by a pragmatic attitude toward the system's ability to provide him with security and upward mobility, the peasant finds himself incorporated within the paternalistic relationship (in both its valoric and subjective aspects).

In general terms, then, we can venture the hypothesis that paternalism has two different but complementary faces. One of these consists of a series of stimuli and responses that tend to create identification of and subjugation to the image of the *patrón* as an indispensable element for the functioning of the estate and the personal security of the *campesino*. The other face is related to the worker himself and his eagerness to use the relationship for his personal benefit. The degree to which the latter phenomenon manifests itself will depend on the type of consciousness the peasant possesses. If, for example, he confuses the image of the *patrón* with the hacienda system in such a way that he himself identifies with the *fundo* through the patronal image, the result will be a static paternalism. On the other hand, if the image of the *patrón* is separate from that of the *fundo* and is perceived only as an element necessary for the functioning of the *fundo*, then the form of paternalism will be less passive and will take on a more utilitarian character in which the *patrón* is "used" by the peasantry.

These forms of paternalism reflect different ways in which the hacienda functions as a power structure. In the first case the peasant is part of a clientele without demands of his own and subject to a thoroughgoing arbitrariness on the part of the *patrón*. This type of situation requires workers with a low educational level, in an exploitive economic and social system that is closed to external influences. Paternalism of the second type works as a defense of the *patrón*, who is seen as a support of the peasant's status as a marginal market farmer. In this case the peasant does not compromise himself to the point of jeopardizing the position he has acquired—especially when he has a chance to maintain that position regardless of the fate of the landowner. This is the case of D, for whom the owner is most important as a guarantee of personal security; but when the *patrón* is ousted, D opts for the type of tenure that will give him security and allow him to develop the status he has attained on the hacienda— independent work as a small farmer.

This type of peasant (*apatronado*) can exert a great deal of pressure toward deciding the eventual distribution of the land in small holdings. If the *apatronados* succeed in gaining some influence over the other sectors of the peasantry with whom they have no great differences, they may become the pressure group that leads the peasantry into such a system of land tenure. Once again, then, we are faced with the problem of the heterogeneous composition of the peasantry as a class that may be oriented in different directions according to the strata that assume leadership.

It is obvious that if leadership is gained by the type of peasant represented by D or, to a certain degree, by N, there is a risk of distorting the process of agrarian reform as a mechanism for distributing the power and wealth of the land. Such peasants, when they become owners, will open the way to a new stratification based upon new relations of economic dependence characterized by a large mass of salaried workers and relatively few landowners.

The Follower

Like the two preceding cases, C was born and raised on the *fundo*. Unlike them, however, he worked for some time outside the *fundo* in neighboring *comunas*. Yet in spite of this experience he knows few people outside the hacienda and he never leaves the *fundo* except for his monthly shopping visits to Melipilla. At present he belongs to no political organization. He participates in the meetings of the union but has no official responsibilities of leadership.

As is the case with the majority of the peasants, the setting in which C's consciousness develops is severely limited. He has practically no contacts with the outside and lacks a broad network of social relations. The change that the takeover has worked in him may be seen in his participation in the new organization for managing the *fundo*. This participation leads him into some activity outside his routine, but it is not paralleled by the development of any new consciousness.

C's changes in attitude are not determined by the development of consciousness but by the acceptance of a new leadership. This seems to be a basic characteristic of his attitude toward the new circumstances in which his own ability and decision to adapt are transferred to the new leaders. This attitude is clear in the position he takes toward the union: "Of course it's good that there is a union, but I don't really know how it is or if it has advantages." He does not hesitate to give his support to the union, because he believes what it tells him.

When he is asked about the causes of the takeover he shows the discrepancies between his conduct and the development of his consciousness. In comparison with what one might conclude from his actions, his consciousness seems to be quite undeveloped. This characteristic will be studied from different points of view.

In the first place, C's reaction to the *patrón* is dominated by the image he has developed of him; this image revolves around the question of *regalías*. "The *patrón* we had here was the worst possible. He didn't fulfill his obligations to us. He only gave us a cuarto of land as *regalía*, and, since I was a master carpenter, I had a right to one and a half cuartos. But he only gave me one. So here I was working just one cuarto and making a tiny salary." His negative image is restricted to this single *patrón*, however. "Not all of the *patrones* are like that—there are better ones, much better ones. But in his case the situation couldn't go on. Never."

C's negative attitude therefore seems to be conditioned by the restriction of his *regalías* and by a feeling of frustration because his status as a skilled worker entitled him to more payment than he received. The curtailment of *regalías* was an obstacle to his economic progress as well as an attack on his internal status. A sense of social frustration, then, was added to the impact of more severe exploitation.

C clearly holds the belief that it is no longer possible to solve his problems through the *patrón*; that an impasse has been reached in their relationship. He has arrived at the critical point where new decisions must be made. But he does not generalize the crisis, which remains limited to and oriented by the concept of the "bad *patrón*." C cannot be said to have formed a clear notion of the existence of a generalized exploitive relationship between the peasantry and the owners. His dominant idea is that his *patrón* does not fulfill his obligations to the peasants, but that there are others who do: "...if the *patrón* had treated the *inquilinos* well, we wouldn't have done anything." Continuing with this logic, C feels that it is bad for other peasants to want to take the *fundos* of good owners: "But if they have a good *patrón* they shouldn't do it." Obviously a good *patrón* is one who is generous with *regalías*, and C does not support the peasants against "good" owners: "...if the *patrón* is good to them then it's unjust, and they shouldn't try to bother him."

The patronal image is of obvious importance as long as the peasant, under normal conditions, seeks a "good *patrón*" under whom he can develop freely. But after the takeover, the peasant's position on the *fundo* undergoes a violent transformation. Suddenly he affirms his new status as a marginal entrepreneur and does not wish to return to the patronal system: "It is better to work for yourself than for a *patrón*. That's how I'd prefer it."

The idea of the good *patrón* being determined by distribution of *regalías* explains why C evaluates the level of his exploitation in terms of the *regalías* he receives. The *regalía* becomes the frame of reference against which payments are weighed and aspirations defined. "Yes, when Marín was *patrón*, there were some people here who had more than others. . . . we call them *amarillos* [yellow]. They've never pulled their own weight; they've never gone along with us." The social frustration involved creates a certain aggressiveness against these privileged peasants who were able to reach the status toward which C aspires.

The latent conflict with these *amarillos* (the *empleados*) gives cohesion to the group that feels discriminated against. The reaction provoked by pure economic exploitation is intensified by the existence of this privileged group. We must conclude, then, that it is primarily the peasant's status as a marginal entrepreneur or market farmer on the hacienda that determines the orientation of his behavior and the nature of his aspirations. His simple condition as a worker seems to be secondary.

This fact becomes still more obvious when C refers to the causes of the movement to take the *fundo*. He begins by speaking of the small salaries paid by the *patrón* and the fact that the *patrón* held back part of the peasants' salaries. "We started to complain one time when Don Eduardo [Marín] held the money back because of something to do with the animals we had. That was when we got some life in us and began to protest. We called a strike here—we didn't want to work." This is the predominant factor in the development of C's consciousness, because when the *patrón* gives him *regalías* and privileges, there is no conflict of interests. The opposition of interests between the *patrón* and the *inquilino* in his status of marginal farmer is aggravated by the gradual loss of this status and the *inquilinos'* transformation into salaried labor. The contradiction is not between the patronal sector and salaried labor, but between those peasants who resist the loss of their status as marginal agricultural entrepreneurs and the circumstances that cause the change. Consequently, the greatest political dynamism of the peasantry is found in those who are undergoing a transformation in their status rather than in those who are merely reduced to economic exploitation within the same status they have always had.

Nevertheless, when the process of transformation to salaried labor is slowed down or stopped by the *patrón's* concession of the indispensable *regalías* and other privileges, a parallel process of decomposition of the patronal structure is set in motion. The *patrón* begins to lose prestige, and the idea grows that it is perfectly possible to do without the *patrón* in the working of the *fundo*. This perception is not the result of a conflict of antagonistic interests, but the simple outgrowth of the fact that the *inquilinos* have partially or totally substituted themselves in the place of the *patrón*. Culiprán is an example of a case in which the *fundo* has reached such a level of decomposition of the patronal economy. In such cases, the continuance of the *patrón* is in name only and is explained by his functionality in the system of *regalías* so important to an *inquilino* like C, and by the lack of a clear perception that the system can indeed function stably without a *patrón*. For C, then, the most important thing is the *regalías* provided by the *patrón*; if this condition is fulfilled, C's antagonism is not sufficient to lead him into a confrontation with the landowner.

The difference between this case and that of D is that for D the *regalía* system of mutual obligations and duties functioned well (probably at the cost of not functioning for other peasants). Nevertheless, both D and C differ from N in that only the latter seeks the destruction of the *regalía* system, while D and C would have remained within that system. But since all three occupy the same status, their final aspirations are identical.

The most important thing for C, then, is not to eliminate the *patrón* but to secure benefits. This attitude does not mean that he thinks the *patrón* is indispensable, but it shows that he is indifferent to the question as long as the system continues to function. Therefore, when the *patrón* fails or is eliminated as distributor of privileges or *regalías*, C replaces him by the concept of private ownership: "I'd rather have them give us each a piece of land."

C feels that the success of the movement depended on two factors: external help and the unity of the peasants of Culiprán. Of the outside aid received, he says: ". . . we felt that everyone supported us because senators and deputies had come from Santiago. There were plenty of leaders from Santiago to protect us. . . . Don Manuel Muñoz was the one who organized that movement. He's from Santiago, from Puente Alto. When could we have done it alone? Never." In this attitude C agrees with the leader (N) who also insisted that the most important factors were the outside help from Santiago and the internal unity of the peasants.

This unity takes the form of mutual protection mixed with a capability of physical aggression. "Of course we could have stopped the *patrón* with just our own people because we were united. There were enough of us here for that—two hundred and seventy or eighty."

C became conscious of these two elements of the movement's success at the time of the confrontation with the police—his first experience of peasant solidarity. For the first time the peasantry saw the meaning of collective action and became aware of their own strength. "So the whole thing was over right there [the confrontation]. We had confidence because we were all united."

It is extremely important to understand that the development of group consciousness takes place after the beginning of the movement itself, and that it arises as a result of external aid. It is true that the confrontation with authority gave the movement a certain independence from this aid, but the new consciousness was not sufficiently dynamic to maintain the action of the peasant group without outside help.

Another aspect worthy of consideration is the feeling of security that accompanies the presence of group consciousness. Such security is dependent upon a minimum strength of the participants and therefore requires broader participation in the case of small peasant groups (for example, cooperation by the peasants of several *fundos*).

Broader solidarity can only be brought about if (1) the peasant actually wants to go beyond the borders of his *fundo*; (2) the social composition of the peasantry in the different *fundos* is more or less similar so that the workers involved may broadly share the same aspirations; and (3) the nature of their relations with the *patrón* and the system itself creates the conditions necessary for similarly oriented movements. Given the tendency to see the *regalía* system as a criterion for the stratification of landowners as "good" or "bad," however, it is difficult for the peasants to reach a common perception of their different *patrones*. The special characteristics of each *fundo* predominate, and the question of quality and quantity of *regalías* continues to overshadow the exploitive relationship to which the peasant is subjected.

One means of determining the degree to which the peasant has developed a group consciousness that transcends the boundaries of the *fundo* is to find out how he perceives the effect that the Culiprán experience has had on the rest of the peasantry, and what opinion he holds about the possibility of these other peasants repeating the feat: "You ask if the takeover on Culiprán has influenced the neighboring *fundos*? Yes. For example, they've become enthusiastic. . . . Of course all the neighbor *fundos* have been organized by this *fundo*. . . . Still, I think there are too few in Popeta to do the same thing we did here." The people of Culiprán are conscious of having taken the initiative, and feel that the other sectors should learn from their experience. But this feeling of serving as an example is limited by the inhibition against supporting those peasants who have a "good *patrón*," and by doubts about the possibility of duplicating the experience of Culiprán, because "there are too few . . . to do the same thing we did here."

C's opinions always take individual *fundos* as a reference—*fundos* with which he has some relation through relatives, friends, or acquaintances. He exhibits a sense of differentiation that is typical of a man who feels himself to be part of an action that is worthy of imitation, but who will do nothing on his own to stimulate such imitation. The informant is supported by a new sense of security that is the result of his newly defined status. This is not to say that he finds himself in a completely structured situation, but C's position is beginning to crystallize now that the obstacles have been destroyed. Without considering the forms that land tenure may finally take, he shows himself satisfied with the new system and the work itself. "I am better off now, although who knows how things will turn out. Anyway, the small farms [chacras] are working better now."

The reason behind this satisfaction is the elimination of the privileged sectors and the discrimination and frustrations to which C was subjected. "It is better this way because each one works for himself in the community. Everyone here is eager to work." Still, his attitude toward the land is measured by his desire to have a plot of his own regardless of the loss of Social Security payments that accompanied the elimination of the *patrón*.

For C the desire to earn more and be independent is more important than security, and in this factor he is different from D and similar to N. His is the attitude of a man who for the first time glimpses the possibility of achieving his goals, and for whom anything outside the achievement of these goals is therefore secondary. In this he differs from D, who had already reached his goals before the takeover and who therefore values what he lost. C, on the other hand, only recently has obtained that which D received through the landowner: the possession of a plot of land slightly larger than one cuadra in size.

The desire for land is so deeply ingrained in the peasant that any form of solidarity appears to contradict it. Consequently, the work in community is not possible: "I think we'd all end up fighting." Independence at any price is preferable to the security of the extended and organized group.

But even the incipient experience of collaboration, which C accepts as egalitarian because it demands that everyone, including the *apatronados*, work at the same level, breaks down the image of landownership as the peasants' highest aspiration. Since this egalitarian mentality is associated with the elimination of inequalities or differentiations within the hacienda, it is very important that in any experience of community labor the tensions emanating from internal differences be resolved, whether they are due to the peasants' unequal abilities to work or to other causes. We can venture further by offering the hypothesis that the *inquilino* is oriented toward private property not only because he sees in this the fulfillment of the potential position that he held on the *fundo* (even if the position was quite unstable, as is the case with the marginal farmers), but also because of a reaction to any form of work that maintains the internal relations of social differentiation, whether or not they involve dependency.

To some extent communal labor reminds C of the situation that existed when the *fundo* functioned with a nucleus of privileged members and a large mass of unprivileged *inquilinos*. When these aspects of communal work are associated with the exploitive relations existing before the take-over, they turn the peasant away from community labor and push him toward individual and independent landownership. In the case of C, property is a guarantee that the old dependent relationship will never be re-vived. It is therefore of great importance to educate the *campesino* to distinguish between relationships defined functionally by the different roles needed on the hacienda and those relationships that grow out of social differentiation or the exercise of power. When this awareness is united with peasant pragmatism, the retention of community forms of labor is not difficult. The tendency that many *campesinos* show to opt for private or independent ownership is not precisely a question of preference; it is caused by the rejection of community labor when it is associated with the old hacienda and its inequalities.

In pointing out the most important aspects of C's consciousness, we can see that he exhibits some of the elements of our typology. First, he does not share the paternalistic idea of the *patrón* as indispensable—either to the functioning of the hacienda or as a factor in C's personal security. This is true because he makes the distinction between the *patrón* and the *regalía* system as conditions of work; the *regalía* system is neither confused with nor subordinated to the *patrón*. The power of the *patrón* is not a function of the paternalistic image and the strength of prestige, but of the owner's capacity to satisfy the *regalía* demands of the peasant. The indispensability of the *patrón*, then, is not seen in terms of the patronal image, but in terms of the *regalías* he can produce. When these *regalías* are no longer forthcoming, the patronal figure loses all its effective authority, just as the existence of good *regalías* reinforces his authority.

C shares some traits of trade union consciousness, such as acceptance of organization and pressure-group activism as long as these take place within the confines of the *fundo*. On the other hand, C's consciousness is set apart from the trade union phase by the fact that he adheres to the new situation mainly because of his loyalty to the leaders. The series of changes that he has experienced on the *fundo* (reduction of *regalías*, protests, defeats, petitions, strikes, expulsion of the owner, and the taking of the *fundo*) requires that a new stability be imposed by the leadership. Just as these changes have not been the exclusive results of the spontaneous action of the *campesinos* but of elements from outside the system that guided and encouraged the peasants, neither will the establishment of the new stability be entirely the product of peasant action, but will depend on the leaders themselves—at least during the period of adjustment to new roles.

In the course of the transition to the new role structure, C will submit to the standards dictated by the leaders, especially if he has not yet fully reconciled the reality of these new roles with the mentality that was instilled in him under the old system. In this situation, persons in contact with the outside become the elements that determine the new equilibrium on the *fundo* because the peasants see them as the power factors that made the change possible. This situation may be prolonged until the peasants have structured a new system and have begun to see the leaders as elements that conflict with the functioning of the *fundo*. At this stage they will have effectively freed themselves from the necessity of external supports.

8. Culiprán, Six Years Later

The land colony (*asentamiento*) that was established in November 1965 was worked communally until February 1968, when it was joined to the neighboring colony of Popeta and broken up into small private holdings. The *inquilinos* and *inquilino* sharecroppers of Culiprán and Popeta, and seven families unconnected with either *fundo*, acquired land through the parcelization process. The total land area of 10,500 hectares, of which 2,500 are irrigated land, was divided into 250 plots averaging from 4 to 6 irrigated hectares. The cost of 33,500 escudos includes a house and a fence along the public road and is payable over a thirty-year period with allowance for payment readjustments totalling 50 percent of the rise in the cost of living. The payment aspect has had the effect of turning many *campesinos* against private holdings—even those who were the most ardent supporters of this form of tenure during the communal period. "Everyone wanted his own little plot, but since we had no experience, we didn't know what it would cost us," stated one director of the cooperative.

Nevertheless, some lands continue to be held in common within the sections (*sectores*) of land that have been divided. These communal lands are used primarily for crops requiring extensive cultivation (such as wheat and barley), the pasturing of beef cattle, sheep and dairy herds, and forest reserves. Also, these lands are necessary because "the private plots don't make enough to live on," as one of the peasants admitted.

Three important problems are involved with the new situation: first, the predicament of the children (sons) of the new landholders who have remained on the land to help their parents or to work for others who have no children. They are paid twenty escudos per day,[1] receive their meals free, and are not subject to other charges (*imposiciones*). At the present time (1971), there are some eighty persons laboring under these conditions. Second, the new owners do not want to work their land themselves, preferring to hire wage labor from the population at large. Finally, some of the *parceleros* have succeeded in acquiring more than one plot of land.

Since the breakup of the *fundo*, some fifteen individuals have modernized their holdings by acquiring tractors through the facilities of the CORA and renting them to other *campesinos*. Others own trucks with which they haul produce to Santiago at a special discount of 15 percent for members of the cooperative. The peasants who have succeeded in amassing more capital than the others are those who have obtained more than one plot of land.

The administration of the land colony is divided into sectors, each one with a council and a president. The sectoral presidents together make up the Council of Administration of the cooperative. Each sectoral council controls and provides for the individual plots through its funds and control of utilities, which are divided among the small holders.

Finally, the same peasant pragmatism reflected in the interviews is still evident after the distribution of the land. The same *campesino* who advocated individual plots in spite of his socialist political views now reacts against parcelization, protesting that it has been imposed by the state. Clearly, this peasant's attitude is determined by the fact that the land distribution process has not favored him to the extent of his expectations. He is critical of the location of the different plots, feeling that some *campesinos* have benefitted more than others because of access to roads and the quality of the land. For instance, his own land lacks direct access to the main road, which can only be reached by crossing another man's pasture and a stream spanned by a crude bridge. Another important aspect of his behavior is the concern he feels over not having a secure monthly income, because the payments of the CORA are subject to delays. All this causes the *campesino* to become more oriented toward a form of land

[1] About $1.75 per day, as of October 1970.

tenure capable of assuring him the same stability and security to which he was accustomed under the old paternalistic system. His previous goal of removing the *patrón*, taking his position, and gaining the riches connected to that position begins to collapse when confronted with the evidence that there is no absolute equivalency between the role of *patrón* and an increase in personal wealth. On the contrary, suddenly the *campesino* is faced with a series of tasks and risks, which, because he does not know how to deal with them correctly, may cause his own position to deteriorate along with his commitment to this new form of landholding. The ideal of private property, which was a projection from the hacienda-*patrón* model, is replaced by a model more consistent with the peasant's own experience.

It can be concluded, then, that thinking about the land-tenure model to be adopted passes through two phases: the first is conditioned by the experience of the immediate past when the concept of property is influenced by the system that oppressed the peasant before but is now conceived as the instrument of personal liberation. The second phase consists of a modification of this view as a result of the experience gained as a free agent independent of the traditional exploitive relationship.

These two phases need not be contradictory if some care is taken to prepare for the change of tenure within the broad context of a completely new system of relations and information that opens the *campesino* to the demands and possibilities created by society as a whole. In other words, the *campesino* must be placed within a more complex system of actions and reactions—one capable of overcoming his geographic and social localism and the cultural narrowness that causes this localism. But none of this can be guaranteed by a simple change in tenure or access to the means of production.

9. Epilogue

Six years have now passed since the beginning of the agrarian reform on the *fundo* Culiprán. It is instructive, therefore, to reassess the evolutionary reform process that has created the present situation, and to determine the validity of some of the predictions made in the course of this study, generalizing our prognosis in line with the Chilean peasant movement as a whole.

It can be seen that agrarian reform based on the expropriation of individual *fundos* stimulates the appearance of pressure groups representing the privileged *campesinos* (*asentados*). The mass of *fundo* workers, on the other hand, is marginalized and isolated, causing a loss of peasant solidarity as the division between the *asentados* and the rest of the peasants becomes more evident. The cause of this division within the peasantry is to be found in the reformation of land-tenure structure along lines modeled on the old hacienda system. As we have written elsewhere, "the peasants develop a tendency to identify with the enterprise itself, and are therefore prone to separate into isolated groups unconnected by any effective sense of solidarity."[1] Far from creating any solidarity, the stage of reform consciousness is intensified, "superimposing traditional relations upon the new

[1] Hugo Zemelman Merino, "Factores determinantes en el surgimiento de la clase campesina," *Revista Cuadernos de la Realidad Nacional* (March 1971).

system; tending to integrate the new situation with the old. Because of this, a peasant movement organized on this basis will remain tied to previously learned patterns of paternalism, individualism, exploitation, etc."[2] This maintenance of traditional behavior patterns typifies the land colonies where the peasants have not yet cast off standards of behavior that are disfunctional within the new cooperative or communal patterns of landholding.

It can be further affirmed that, for the peasants interviewed, the transformation from the original status as *inquilino* to that of salaried laborer is crucial in the development of a conflict situation on the *fundo*. Moreover, this factor is also a determinant in the peasant's own thinking about land tenure, for, in spite of the communal nature of property in the first stages after the takeover, peasant attitudes finally become oriented toward parcelization—fulfilling the *inquilino* ideal of transformation into a small property owner. The change from hacienda to land colony is in itself clearly not sufficient to change a peasant mentality forged by generations of existence in a system based on isolation and paternalism. On Culiprán the desire to possess land is so strong that any gesture of solidarity seems to contradict the aspirations of peasants who no longer believe in or feel any peasant solidarity, but rather think that "each one has to look out for himself."

In this connection we present a theoretical framework that was developed from the assumption that the agricultural unit can be considered as a social system. This framework may anticipate some of the conflicts that are now emerging after six years of agrarian reform.[3]

The form of land tenure on the *fundo,* in addition to being viewed from the point of access to land, also constitutes a whole social system characterized by modes of interaction between its component members. The most important characteristic of this social system is its isolation from the rest of society—an isolation that affects the workers especially and influences their behavior, attitudes, and values. Our basic assumption is that the tenure system is characterized by limited possibilities of interaction, both internally and externally—particularly for the peasants who limit themselves within the boundaries of the estate, lacking almost all contact with the outside world. The *inquilino* is especially subject to this isolation because he is burdened by a semiemotional attachment to the estate where

[2] Ibid.
[3] Hugo Zemelman Merino, "El fundo como sistema de interacciones del campesino," *ICIRA*. Document no. 57. (Santiago, 1965).

he resides. The social horizons of the *inquilino* and the alternatives before him are concentrated within the boundaries of the hacienda, and the *patrón* represents the mechanism that maintains stability within the *fundo* and contacts with the outside world. Together these factors create the conditions under which the *inquilino* develops a submissive attitude toward the *patrón*.

The resultant isolation is of the utmost significance, for it reinforces attitudes and habits that inhibit the eventual maturation of a peasant consciousness capable of dealing with unfamiliar situations. It must be remembered that a powerful sense of routine is closely connected with any system of restricted and narrow interactions. The consequent devotion to familiar modes of behavior and the exaggerated importance attached to the *patrón* are among the most important obstacles to adaptation and initiative among the peasantry.

Isolation is the fundamental element in the paternalistic power structure of the estate. Paternalism thrives on the isolation, which accentuates the peasants' feeling of personal dependency on the *patrón*, who, in the absence of points of reference outside the *fundo*, ultimately comes to be seen as a protector figure. Paternalism, then, is one of the prime instruments of power in the worker-*patrón* relation. Thus, it is impossible to liberate the *campesino* from his situation without radically changing the conditions that make this paternalism possible: the first of these conditions is the complete isolation of the peasant. It is not enough to bestow the means of production on the *campesino*, for his lot will not be improved definitively if his possibilities of communication and social contacts are not broadened at the same time.

As the system of land tenure is modified, therefore, it is necessary to incorporate the peasant into organizations that will force him to participate in a broader system of interactions than that affected simply by the changes in land tenure. This fact should underline the immense importance of establishing a concrete policy regarding the communications, information, and relations of the land colony with nearby towns—factors that have seldom been considered a significant part of agrarian reform policy. If we conceive the modification of the tenure system within the context of a policy of gradual urbanization of the rural sector, then it can be seen that the functioning of the new tenure structure is strongly affected by the lack of creative activity by the rural population. Moreover, to the extent that institutional innovations are not balanced by measures that incorporate the rural population in broader social contexts, the result will be a contradictory situation in which a change of the land-tenure system coexists with the traditional attitudes, habits, and behavior of the peasantry. Although the change of the tenure system itself will necessarily produce a modification in the position of the peasant, this modification cannot keep up with the intensity of land redistribution and, therefore, a lag will occur in the transformation of attitudes, values, and conduct. This lag is obvious for the majority of *inquilinos,* who require some modification of the tenure system. A peasant with land of his own can be a serious obstacle to the functioning of the new system if the nature of his participation in national society remains unchanged.

Agrarian reform policy, then, cannot be limited to measures affecting land tenure. An essential part of that policy should be a series of measures designed to urbanize the agrarian sector by considering agrarian reform as only one aspect of a larger policy of modernization of the countryside. This is a natural step from viewing the agricultural estate as a social system, and land tenure as an aggregate of basic (social) institutions. The urbanization of the countryside generally means the incorporation of *campesinos* into situations of interaction that overcome the barriers imposed by the *fundo* system (or by the land colony). To forge this link with the outside world, one must remember that it is the *campesino* himself who will or will not take advantage of the potentials contained in the new institutional structure. The power structure cannot be changed merely by modifying access to the land; it must be subjected to the influence of new forms of interaction among the *campesinos,* and between *campesinos* and the outside world.

The supposition of our argument is that the institutional aspect is not in itself a factor of sufficient dynamism to produce more dynamic attitudes among the peasantry. Definite policies of urbanization are called for— policies capable of promoting a more complete synchronization between the different levels of the process of change. This is a basic assumption because the lack of synchronization between different aspects of the process is the cause of serious disturbances whenever the tempo of institutional change varies greatly from that of cultural change.

If this concept of synchronization is not foremost in policy decisions, the complexity of the process is being ignored and many of the goals of change will be frustrated. We can go a step further by saying that, even when institutional change is the product of group pressure (in this case, by the peasantry), the very agents of this pressure do not adjust to the new system in the broadest sense, but are prone to face these new institutions with attitudes learned from the previous power elite (the *patrones*). In the last analysis, then, the teachings of the old dominant group have not been spent in vain, for the very norms most easily assimilated by the peasant groups are precisely those that were held by their exploiters. The desire to expel the *patrón* is accompanied by a strong tendency to adopt some characteristics of his behavior, which shows the real meaning of the idea that any true agrarian reform must have its own internal dynamics. If we lose sight of this idea as our central orientation, then the process of change will become one of mere social mobility instead of overcoming traditional structures and transforming them into new and dynamic ones. Social mobility may be one of the consequences of agrarian reform, but it cannot furnish either the point of departure or the justification for such a transformation. It must also be clear that none of the problems we are dealing with is of any importance if we conceive of the agrarian reform as a mechanism for the upward mobility of urban or rural middle sectors. Such a conception does not anticipate any real change of the power structure in the *campo,* but rather looks forward to the consolidation of a new dominant stratum that scarcely or not at all modifies the present situation.

If the entire process of agrarian reform is not reoriented in the broad sense described above, it will develop along lines marked by the characteristic elements of the very situation it seeks to overcome. Not only will contradictions appear between the level of structural change and that of consciousness, but also the dynamics of the process will be characterized by the material interests and values of the *campesinos* who were most active on the hacienda before the takeover—those who have lost their previous status as favored beneficiaries of the *regalía* system and who are now inclined to prefer forms of land tenure that can transform them into small holders.

In this study of Culiprán we have shown that even the most active and ideological *campesinos* see the conflict as one leading ultimately to their replacement of the *patrón.* Since this conception does not presuppose any modification of the structure of property, the process of change will evolve within a conservative and traditional framework oriented toward private property. We can conclude that, if the peasant movement is influenced predominantly by the type of *campesino* who has benefitted from the patronal system of *regalías,* the movement will finally develop into a system of isolated pressure groups (*parceleros*). When this development occurs, the conditions will have been created in which new lines of stratification can appear and new forms of exploitation can be erected.

The first phase of agrarian reform (1965-1970) can be outlined in four stages: (1) the formation of privileged groups lacking a sense of solidarity; (2) renewal of old patterns of exploitation, expressed in the tendency of peasants to hire wage labor; (3) the tendency to elevate one's status from *inquilino* to private landholder; and (4) the isolation of these groups from the mass of the peasantry. Due to the course taken by this first phase of agrarian reform, new social tensions have developed.

APPENDICES

A. Interview with a Former Leader of the Peasant Committee

I was born and raised in this very house. I was ten when Arturo Alessandri Palma was elected, and this hacienda was the first to go out on the strike called by the Federación Obrera de Chile [Chilean Workers Federation]. After that we marched to Melipilla. That night—I was ten and shivering from the cold with my parents—we marched. We marched and we gained a little ground. In those days my father was making 80 cobres as an *inquilino* on the hacienda, but after the strike he made 1.20 pesos—they gave him a raise of 40 cobres.

So I grew, and when I reached the age to do military service they also registered me to vote. When the election of the late Aguirre Cerda came along, the Peasant League was formed and I began to work as a leader. We were making 2.50 pesos by then, and they raised us to 3.20. When we got that raise the *patrón* axed a few of the *inquilinos*—Emiliano Gárate was one of them. They were fired for being mixed up in the Peasant League. That was when the Socialists joined us here.

I'm an *inquilino*; I've never done sharecropping—just a worker. Right now we've got something like 250 *inquilinos* living and working here. There's only one that's sharecropped; he's got a little farm near here. The rest are just plain *inquilinos*. *Obligados*, yes, sir. We don't have any *afuerinos* [migrant laborers], either. The ones who came before could work here, but not anymore. It's been around ten years now that they haven't let *afuerinos* in; the real residents of the *fundo* work here—nearly all of them born and raised in Culiprán. The last contracts were made almost forty years ago. Almost all the *inquilinos* have lived here a long time.

I have relatives: cousins and brothers and sisters here and in the neighboring *fundo* in San Miguel. Also in Santiago. My relatives are scattered in at least five different places. I've got two sons and some nephews and so forth in Santiago. I have lots of friends—on the *fundo*, outside, and in Melipilla, too. It's a long way but sometimes we get to visit. Sometimes they come to see me, sometimes I go to see them. Every year a family we know comes. I don't go to Melipilla much, maybe three times a week now; but when there's a campaign and we have to put up posters we're there nearly every day.

The radio and newspapers tell me about what's going on outside, but I don't have a radio right now. The one I had belonged to a relative of mine who took it with him when he went to Mallí; so for the moment I don't get any news. But I'm going to get myself a radio pretty soon. The papers come too—the Socialist paper and *El Siglo*[1] once a week or once a month. *El Siglo* doesn't get here too often. The people who come through are usually relatives—people from Santiago. One of my sisters lives in Barrancas,[2] and they always come to visit every year when we have fruit and watermelons here. They come to dance the *cueca* and eat some of our *pencacitos*. The salesmen come with their trucks to sell things to us.

The *inquilinos* grow corn and peas and potatoes here—all kinds of food. We eat what we need and sell the rest. I made half a million pesos off just what I sold from this field at the Vega Poniente [market] in Santiago; we take it to Santiago for the market because there is no market to speak of in Melipilla.

We have to pay for freight costs—one thousand pesos per sack. Sometimes the cost is split up between several men, other times one man gives me a load of around eighty sacks and pays the freight himself. We do that once a year and I go myself in one of the trucks we have here, like that one parked beside the house.

There are machines on the *fundo*, too. You say you haven't seen any, but that is because they're out working. Not long ago I was with a machine digging ditches for irrigation. I just walk at the side of the ditching machinery giving orders to dig the ditches where they're needed. But up on top there is a driver. The people who work the machines here are all from the *fundo*. In two or three days after they bring us a new machine I can learn to run it; then we give it to one of the young men who learns to run it himself. We do it that way here because the specialists from outside are very expensive.

The things we don't produce ourselves we buy at the *fundo* of Don D. Jorquera near here—about two kilometers away. You go to Melipilla when you have 300,000 pesos saved; then you take them to town and put them to use. With half a million you can buy a little heifer or something like that, but that's pretty rare. Most people go to Melipilla only once a month—twice a month at most. You know, it's fourteen or fifteen kilometers from here to Melipilla. But when we had the meeting over the *fundo*

[1] Communist party daily newspaper.
[2] A municipality of Greater Santiago.

we were going three times a week. We were waiting from May to October. In October we finally got possession of the land.

All the peasants here know agriculture. We know how to plant potatoes and corn, how to plant *poroto* [beans] and watermelon. We know about all that.

As to whether there's been any political organization here, I can tell you there has not. Political parties tried organizing, but the *patrón* tossed them out. We tried to organize ourselves, too. When we had our union set up before, the *patrón* came along with all the humanity of a young billygoat and stopped us from organizing. But now we have our union, the union and the Comité del Asentamiento [Land Tenure Colony Committee, or the Peasant Committee].

I have friends: Socialists who come to teach, to open your eyes and give you the key and lead you down the right road. Earlier when we had problems and no organization to consult, there was a minister[3] who took care of things here. He would come and hear your complaints. He was the one who fixed things then. We couldn't have political parties because they threw us out. We had a union here before, when the minister of commerce was that man ... I forget his name ... Oscar Schnake,[4] yes, it was then. But to ask to organize anything here, well, five years ago in March we tried. That was when I read in a paper about Alessandri's agrarian reform. I called my *compañeros* together but they didn't believe me—they never did at first. But I got them together and said: "This is what's happening, *compañeros,* and this is what we are going to have to do." Later we met again, and I talked to them again, and finally some believed me. Pretty soon they were even telling my little daughters about the agrarian reform in the schools—even those little kids [*cabritas*] heard about it; all my little kids heard about the agrarian reform while they were getting educated. And finally the *empleados* and the boss even heard of it. The *patrón,* Don Ligualdo, knows me very well. One day when he was working here I came up and he greeted me before I reached him. "What's up, Lafferte,"[5] he said, because the administrator always called me Lafferte. He didn't know that I was a Socialist. "What's new, Lafferte, did you know that there was a bill in the Chamber of Deputies last night and you were beaten; and so was that *compañero* of yours." That was back when they took the island from Fidel Castro.[6] We were shucking corn in those days, before the crop was all in, and he said: "What happened to your

[3] The administrator of the *fundo* was called *ministro,* or minister.
[4] Oscar Schnake, Socialist minister during the presidency of Pedro Cequirre Cerda, 1939-1941.
[5] Lafferte was a famous Communist leader.
[6] U.S.-sponsored invasion of Cuba, April 1961.

compañero Fidel Castro, who they've got surrounded? Tomorrow you're going to find out that he is dead."

"Maybe so, Don Luis," I said, "maybe so, but I don't think there's any man more clever than Fidel Castro on this earth." I almost bet him. Then the next day I went to the movie in San Manuel—the one where Fidel is riding on a burro. Then, since the United States itself had given him . . . what do you call it? artillery that couldn't reach the airplanes— machine guns and mortars and all that, but they couldn't reach the planes, we said: "Now they're going to finish him because his arms aren't good enough." Then when Fidel goes the next day and the airplanes attack—it was in a film when the one giving orders said: "Let's get out, *compañeros*! These are Soviet arms—not ours!" The next day I saw the *patrón* again and when he met me he said: "Hombre, that was great, what he did. Fidel really kicked them around, he took them all prisoners." I said: "You see," and I shook his hand, "was I right or not?"

The most important thing I've done here is to get the *compañeros* to- gether and encourage them—at least during the takeover. The Christian Democrats didn't want us to take the land. They didn't want it at all. Then the Socialist leaders came to talk with me.

It was very hard to get the people's enthusiasm, but finally they came around. Sometimes the son of the minister used to come here—to where we worked, in ditches like that, and everyone stopped when we started to talk politics. We started a conversation, and right away he wanted to talk politics with me. He got mad sometimes and started to chew me out, but I said: "Don't get mad, we're just talking. Why get excited if it's just talk?" He would leave laughing. "Just as long as you remember I'm boss," he'd say, but when we got to talking again, he'd get mad again. "Don't get so upset, Don Luis," I said. "Now we have to beat you—once and for all we will have to win."

Do you know when the people began to get enthusiastic? It was when we elected Máximo Venegas deputy. Don't you remember, back then in the year that Aguirre Cerda was president? Well, the Socialists came in here then and we all joined together and had an understanding. We went up into the hills and cut some little clubs with a big saw. So everybody carried one of these clubs. Then when the election came we just put the ballot in the envelopes—they gave us those ballots in the Secretariat. So I carried my vote for Aguirre Cerda here with me. This fellow A. G. came out from Melipilla. He was still a young guy then. When I saw him for the first time I said: "Listen, I know you. You were in the Falange Nacional before. It looks to me that you're in with the right wing." "No, hombre," he said, "no, no, now I'm a leftist."

But after Aguirre Cerda we lost everything because the *patrón* started to break up the organization and make it hard for the people who didn't go along. I was lucky because he always had respect for me and didn't give me much trouble. But I never betrayed my *compañeros* for him. Since the *patrón* knew that I already had political leaders who could talk to me, he let me off easy—and that saved me. Part of my support was from people of the Socialist party. I have organized and gathered people from the beginning, and I still do. When the takeover came, Don N. Muñoz was already with us here and we all got together in a house, over there. We came into contact with Muñoz through the Christian Democrats, because we were making 840 pesos here then, and a new law said the minimum salary for us to earn was 3,375 pesos, and Muñoz had come to see that the law was enforced. Then the *patrón* came around and took away our free pasture rights [*talaje*] and charged us 9,000 pesos. He let us have only half a cuarto of land instead of the full cuarto and rented us the other half. That was 10,000 pesos. Then 20,000 for pasture and 10,000 for a load of firewood brought the total to 30,000.

There used to be a few here who were sharecroppers [medieros] because they owned livestock and farm tools, or had more children than the others. When they had a little cash—500,000 pesos or so, they'd buy a cow or a mare that they'd breed and build up their animals that way. Now almost everybody has animals and sharecrops. There must be about 110 who have a couple of mules. I have four right now. They were the ones *papá* left me when he died. We divided up the animals he left and I got one of them. The *inquilinos* never had mules before, but now almost all of them do—since they had the auction of the *fundo* stock. The reason many of us had no mules before was that those who had the biggest families— like me, with eleven kids—couldn't make it with the 400, 500, or 600 pesos we were getting. Last year we made 640 pesos. That is why I had only one team before the auction. It is true that some of the *inquilinos* here have more than others; but they were *empleados* and overseers. It was easy for them to have animals—sheep, cattle, and so forth. If they have five cows and breed them, in a year they have five calves and it makes their lives pretty easy. They even have chickens and can pick up some cash that way. They have tremendous fields. Some have a whole cuadra, and in one cuadra you can make a couple of million pesos. I've only got one-half cuadra now and sometimes they have more than one cuadra—some as many as twenty. They were the ones who became administrators and overseers because it was a family thing. If my father had been an *empleado*, when he died everything would have gone to his son. That was how they did it—through the family and through the *patrón*, too, because the *patrón* could make whoever he wanted an *empleado*.

Before the takeover, the administrator, Don Ligualdo, took care of the problems that came up. We met with him every month, and, if there was trouble with an *inquilino* or something, he decided the problem; and if there was a crime involved it went before the judge. But the administrator was in charge of fixing these things with us individually. If it was a problem where money was needed, he would go to the *patrón* and see about getting that. Once a mare of mine was stolen and it was like I had to buy her back, because the *patrón* loaned me twenty thousand pesos so I could go and look for the horse. She turned up in Paine a month later, so it was almost like buying her again. I spent forty thousand to get her back. All we could do was try to make a deal with the *patrón*. You don't think we could just get a bunch of us together and go up to the boss and say, "*Compañero*, this is what has happened to me and I want you to give me a couple of thousand pesos, and a couple more for my friend here." That way we could have gotten a little money together for our problems, but we couldn't do that. All you could do was to work things out with the *patrón* [administrator]. I've always been an *inquilino*, but I've always thought that a person could do more. What I have always wanted is to make money and have a better life. To own a little bit of land where I am boss—some money and eight cuadras to work with my sons. I already have an opportunity because I have a friend who says that I don't have to kick in with anything and he'll open an account for me in the bank. Then, he says: "If you need livestock I'll buy them and we'll fatten them on your land and then I'll sell them for you. If it costs you two million pesos and we sell for twenty millions, we'll split five apiece." He's a business man who lives in Melipilla—you talked with his brother here.

I'd also like for my sons to be farmers and make some money, because you always know that agriculture is going to go up, and if you have a good year with farming you can make millions. If I had a little tractor and five cuadras to work, I guarantee that, if those five cuadras are good land, then even with corn alone I can make 15 million; and if I spend five I still have ten left.

Everyone has always gotten together here when there are elections; they come to vote for the left, because the people of Culiprán have always been leftist. That was one good thing about the *patrón*, Don Eduardo Marín—he never told us who to vote for. He let us do what we wanted and so we always voted for the left. Everyone made up his own mind.

There are grudges too—I'm involved in one here with a fellow who was president of the party here. He is my cousin, and he's jealous because they always come to see me first. When we had the meeting at the time of the takeover they came to talk to me—right away they'd ask for me. The major of the *carabineros* also asks to talk to me. So that's why they are jealous of me and even want to throw me out of the Directorate. They don't want me in the Directorate or in the Committee either. But I've given them plenty of lessons and so they nominated me and elected me a second time.

Since everything is spread out here, we meet where they distribute the bread—in the morning in the houses where they divide up the bread. There we give orders to the workers. One goes off to work over there, another goes over here, this one goes to the mill, that one to the Los Maitenes pasture, another to Peumo, and so on. You also tell them about meetings there. If you want to meet at such and such a time, you tell them then and they show up. Now that there is a union we have a standing meeting on Thursdays—one at the *paltos,* others over there, others here at Molino. That's how people know about the meetings. The meetings are every Thursday but we also get together in our *compañero's* house to talk every afternoon. That has worked out well because we've always met there since 1920, since Alessandri's massacre of Iquique.[7] I don't know why it has always been there, but we met in that very place in the time of the Federación Obrera, in 1920, when we had to fight.

We have developed a plan for the work that needs to be done here. They always come to ask me because I have more experience. All of this land here, for example, is great for wheat. We're going to cut all those big bramble bushes right down to the water and let them dry up like kindling. Then when they're good and dry we'll clear some of it off and burn the rest. In a few days the fire will leave it nice and bare.

We think we should work as a community. We want to work as a community for two years or three years until we get settled through the land-tenure colony (*por el asentamiento*).[8] Afterward we will divide the land up. But if we don't get along well we won't divide anything. I think our people want the division because each one wants his own little plot. I'm for dividing it up. You see, I have some sisters in Santiago. They've told me that when I have a little bit of my own land they will bring me a tractor to work it, and with a tractor and five or eight cuadras, I'll make it pay. I have a young son and a nephew who is a truck driver in Santiago who will go in with me.

As for Marín, the *patrón,* his main defect was that he was one of the worst *patrones* in Chile. Listen, when they were paying *inquilinos* 1,200 pesos in other places, he was still giving us only 600 pesos per day; he never came around at Easter or at New Years, or even during the year to

---

[7] Refers to government of President Arturo Alessandri's massacre of nitrate workers in the city of Iquique.

[8] Under the agrarian reform law the expropriated farm is worked collectively for three years, after which the peasants vote to either continue working it collectively or divide it into individual plots.

ask: "How are my *inquilinos*? Is there anything you need?" Never. Just rules and politeness and more rules while he took away from us whatever he could. So he kept taking things from us, and all of a sudden he doesn't want to give us any land at all anymore. We even had to pay for the land we used: 10,000 pesos per month for one cuarto—that's 120,000 pesos every year. And even if he hadn't had any faults, naturally it's better to be working on your own land than on somebody else's. What we want to do here is to work. With only one or two cuadras of land—like the overseers used to have—we can make a living. I have a cousin who raises cattle, and with one cuadra he can make three million a year. I tell you, a man can do more—it depends on his ambitions. And you see how fast the money goes nowadays. Well listen, we aren't the only ones with this problem. I think all Chile is feeling it. All Chile. I think that almost all the *patrones* are like this Marín. The first one that fell was this one they kicked out, Catán. Catán and Marín are the same. They're the same because when we went to see X at the CORA, he told us that Catán and Marín were the same. I know some *patrones* around here. I know a few, and I can tell you that something big is going to happen here—something very big. They are all watching us because the people of Culiprán are going to own the land. If I went to the neighboring *fundo* here and explained that to them, they'd come right over.

If you ask my opinion about whether there should be a *jefe* [chief or leader], I think there have to be *jefes;* there is even a *jefe* here. But he isn't able to look after the whole *fundo* himself (he's that cousin of mine I was telling you about—the one who is jealous of me). There used to be an administrator, a manager, and so forth, but now he has to do it all himself. There is just one *jefe,* and another in the CORA. They have to bring *jefes*—then the *fundo* will run smoothly.

That is how it always has to be. And I tell you that even in Santiago—in the towns—there has to be a *jefe.* Here, I think that there always ought to be a man in charge of the farmers. There is one in Culiprán Bajo. He goes to each plot and says, "You have to plant potatoes here, do this there, plant that here." He tells them what they should plant.

You ask how we came to agreements among ourselves. My opinion is that the *compañeros* should meet, and each one give his own opinion, and when they are united that way, the *compañeros* can demand things from the *patrón.* If you're the *patrón* and you don't give in, then we put some pressure on you. "Tomorrow we'll strike, we won't work tomorrow." That is my idea of how to do it. And the other peasants from other places—I've already told you that they are keeping an eye on what we do. It won't take much, one just has to give them a little push and they'll find out right away. I even have a little speech for that. All I have to do is read it to them and they'll see how to call the strike. The first thing is to get them together. Then I can take the leader of the federation that led us and they'll find out how to make petitions and take them to court. "First the petition, *compañeros,* I tell them, "and then we form the unions, and after that when everything is planned out, if the *patrón* still doesn't give in, we'll take the land. And even if the police come out, the peasants know they're not going to kill anybody and that we have people on our side. Even if they don't have anyone to lead them, some *compañero* will come forward and make himself leader—whether he is known from the newspapers or the radio or just as a *compañero.* It's just like we were talking about: while they are making the plans the *compañeros* get to talking together and they themselves decide: "Look, this fellow has more experience than the rest of us. We're going to elect you to lead us, *compañero.*" The smartest one, right? That's how he's elected. Afterward, the union is formed and dues are paid. We pay two thousand a month here. You have to go to all the meetings. I am the secretary and I have to go to the meeting and say, "The meeting in Culiprán is set for such and such a date." You see, the meeting begins at a certain time, and when the session begins we announce the next meeting as well.

The things that we need most are tractors—tractors we can borrow. Also, aside from seed, we are going to need plows, yokes, bolts, scythes, shovels, sickles, and so on. All the things that we are running out of.

If you ask me what kind of persons we are going to need, I would ask myself in the meeting, so that the list of what we are going to need could be made. The problem is that we don't have a cooperative here to bring us goods: canvas, plows, rope, bolts, and everything we'd need for a cooperative.

You ask if we would rather have an agronomist here or someone to teach us about politics. We already have an agronomist. He is a party agronomist, but even if there were no party agronomist here, I would still prefer to have a political leader: one who is a politician—a politician more to the left than to the right. We don't really need an agronomist because we . . . well, just look at me, I'm sure that I could put him in the shade. He would look bad beside me because right here I have three of the best agronomists [his sons] who ever walked. The worst pasture we had—everyone crossed themselves when they went by because it was just a lot of black mud and rocks. Now it's in corn—they make it give top production and it was the worst field here.

The other *campesinos,* from what my friends and relatives around here tell me, are very preoccupied with what we've done. They're already beginning to do the same things we did. They are holding meetings, and even the *campesinos* of the San Manuel *fundo,* where there is a very good *patrón,* are already having meetings. I don't want to get involved in that, because their *patrón* was good to us during the takeover. The eight days of the takeover, when we were on strike, he brought us material for posters and the banners that said "land for those who work it." That's why I haven't wanted to push the people of his *fundo* as long as no one else from here does it. But now that they've been taught a little bit they are going to rise up. I was with one of the men from CORA and he told us that if a *patrón* has fifty cuadras of wheat—more than is good—if there are fifty cuadras of wheat they have to expropriate the *fundo.* Then they are in a situation where they can expropriate it.

I think that they just might take over that *fundo.* They have to be brave if they're going to, because there are many who aren't going to think the way we do. Some will stay with the *patrón.* There are a lot of people on the side of the *patrón* there, and others who don't care. But many are with the workers. I'd like to go by there one of these days and see what I can do.

Up to now the organization we have has gotten along well. The only problem is a football club that has another leadership. So they want to stay off by themselves—they want to get out of the union because they pay dues to their club. But all of us here are with the union and we are going to keep them in the union, too. The leader of the Federation told us that they couldn't pull out, that we all have to obey the union and the union has to control the club, too. So everyone is agreed on that because we need money. There was not even one Christian Democrat before, but with one activist they started to spread, and in the polls, if you can imagine it, they got sixty-seven votes, those Democrats.

Sure, I think the only way the *campesinos* have to solve their problems is to take the *fundos.* That's the only problem. I can't believe that the president is going to say to the *campesinos,* "I'm going to give you an agrarian reform here." You have to take the *fundo* for that. And even if the owners organize against us, like you say they did in Curicó, the people will always fight them. They'll always be up against all the people.

In our case, well, we closed the gates when there were *carabineros* near. Three *carabineros,* and we were in here with the gates locked up tight. They came with a jeep and three trucks with about twenty *carabineros.* So what did we do? Two hundred of us came out; some with rifles, others with shotguns, revolvers, sickles, pikes. We came like a bunch of demons and when they saw us they moved their trucks back so that we could tie the gates shut. When they saw us coming, at night, all together in a tremendous crowd like that, they took off and didn't do anything to us. That's why I believe that it's necessary to stand up to them. And if for some reason they came and wouldn't go back, then we'd attack them and throw them out then and there, and they'd lose their best men.

Of course I think that the *campesinos* have to have help in this. There has to be a minister or deputy who is on our side in the fight, because the plans have to be well made, because, listen—if the plan is badly made, I think we could be killed. If we hadn't gone to Santiago to study the plan three days before, then it wouldn't have worked. It worked because we did what we did. Altamirano[9] came out on the morning of the takeover to verify that we had occupied the land, because he couldn't very well talk to Leighton, the minister of the interior, before we'd taken over, could he? So that when we took the *fundo,* early in the morning, he talked to Leighton. We were here eight days, and there were women here, too. My daughter and a neighbor woman made food for the common pot.

The *patrón* was very refined, very sensitive. Once on an Eighteenth[10] when my mother was coming to visit from Santiago, the *patrón's* administrator, Don Ligualdo, came and walked right in here to the patio and said that there were two jugs of wine. He came into the room with his *carabineros* and took the jugs. Right then I was coming home from work and I saw them breaking the jugs with clubs. So I said to one of the *carabineros:* "Listen, Señor Carabinero, how do you allow these things? Tomorrow is the Eighteenth and we have visitors from Santiago and now you've broken the wine jugs." He said, "Someone told Don Ligualdo that you were up to no good." And I told him, "Whatever I break I pay for." When was he going to pay us for the jugs he broke? That's how the administrators and the owners were. Not now. Now we've taken the land. When we took over we would sit on his porch and listen to the radio. The people went into his house and read the papers—they even stayed in the house of that man who was so arrogant before. By then he had already run to Melipilla because he found out during the night that we were going to take the land. He went to Santiago. He went to see the Chilean team play because he's a fan. Marín never was able to leave. We left him locked up on the other side.

Sure, some of the people were afraid. There were some whose knees were knocking, sure, but not me. I had kids and all, but do you think I was worrying about my *señora*? I wasn't thinking of anyone. We just took a couple of swallows of wine and we were ready—we kept right on tying and fastening [the barricades]. Some of the women cried; many of them were really frightened. At night they didn't sleep because they thought they could already hear shots. I was with a group over there that fired a few times in the air—if the women heard that, who knows what they might have thought? But we said nothing to the women. We only told them when they started to find out from each other after we finally told them

[9] A Socialist senator.
[10] September 18 is Chilean Independence Day.

we wouldn't be home that night. Some of the *compañeros* told them something about it then, and they passed [the news] on from one to another.

That's how our fight was. At first the Christian Democrats told us that they'd give us support, but they didn't deliver. They didn't even bother to come. So we took the *fundo* by ourselves, with the help of two from Santiago; there were two men from Santiago with us. If we hadn't had them, or the support of the politicians, I don't think the people would have had the courage to take the land. They were the ones who came to give us encouragement and make all the plans. Sure some people's knees were knocking.

I had already told the mayor five times: "Look Señor Mayor" (he had our petitions, remember), "if you don't meet our demands and act on our petitions, Señor Mayor, we are going to take the *fundo*. And if the Christian Democrats put us off like they've been doing, then we'll get support from the Confederación de Trabajadores Indígenas de Chile,[11] and we'll take the land." He didn't want us to take the *fundo*; even the CORA people themselves tried to scare us off. "Don't take the *fundo*," they said, "because if you do you'll lose everything you've worked for—you won't have anything." They didn't want us to take it, either. And how can I believe that the president himself is going to come here or to the other *fundos* and make our agrarian reform for us? When? Do you think they're going to do anything to us because we took the land? Well, we're just going to hold onto it here.

They used to make us an eight-day work contract here. At the time of our other fight they gave me eviction papers and they tried to kick me out. I didn't want to sign the paper and they only gave you two or three days to get out. So that when I went to the inspector of labor afterward, he said, "Now all you can do is work." I worked the eight days, and then we went to the inspector and told him what was happening. Then we went to Santiago. He talked to Don Eduardo Marín to tell him that he couldn't do that—after all the things he's let Marín get away with—even throwing other *compañeros* out of the *fundo*. Now he was trying to cut us off, too. He had no right. So the eviction was canceled and I stayed and they had to hire me. All that was during the presidency of Gabriel Gonzales Videla [1946-1952]. I never had that problem again. What they did was to put me to work on the hardest jobs. They put me in the mill and I had to carry 120 kilo sacks up to the top floors. They were trying to punish me, but I could do it and I carried those sacks up there, that's all. They also made me plow with mules instead of the work I was doing here before. But I stayed calm and I took it.

[11] Communist-and-Socialist-led peasant confederation.

If you ask me, I think we're better off now. I really think so. Before we were all very poor. I know people who put their mattresses on the ground to sleep. Now in almost all the houses there is a bronze bedstead. The poverty is not like it was.

I have great hopes for the future. This *compañero,* Gonzales, says that in three years he can guarantee that I'm going to have more than five million pesos. Guaranteed—in three years. "I'm going to get you animals that cost me three million," he says, "and sell them at six, and you'll come out well at harvest time." He told me that.

You ask what I'd think if all the *fundo* owners in Chile disappeared. Well, if they disappear the people will be much better off, because the owners will have to go to the city. They'll go to the towns, and on the *fundos* the people who made them rich will be working for themselves. The money that the rich men made is going to be for the worker. I don't think anyone will be poor—only the lazy ones.

B. Interview with an *Empleado* Who Opposed the Takeover

You ask if you can record? Go right ahead.

Was I for the takeover of the *fundo*? Ha! I guess not. Naturally I didn't dare to leave when I saw that they had locks on the gates. I couldn't anyway, because the people were very aggressive—they had to be aggressive to convince themselves that they could take the *fundo*. This business of doing away with the *patrones* and turning the land over to the *campesinos* . . . well, I don't think it's a bad thing—it's always good to have land to work—but it is not right to take the owner's *fundo*. I don't know what the *patrón* thinks about this, with things the way they are. It's not that I'm scared to say what I think, but look: if you can show that a planter is using his *fundo* badly, fine; in that case it's all right to take it away from him and give it to someone else. But if he is a good farmer, then there's no reason to take it away.

If I were the *patrón* I wouldn't give land to the workers, either. I would give them some land to work so they'd stay on as workers, and I'd give them more *regalías,* of course. It's not that they don't know how to do the work here. They know the land and the work and what should be planted, but what I'm saying is that, if they take that *fundo* from the owner, there will probably be difficulties—like not respecting their leaders. That would be a real problem. People from here—from the *fundo*—would have to be in charge because outsiders don't know our problems. They'd have to be from here even if they didn't have the prestige of the *patrón.* They say that production will drop if there is no agrarian reform. I do think that a solution has to be found for that.

But I was not in favor of this [the takeover]. I'm sixty years old, but there are many old men with the *campesinos* now, and there are others who aren't. I would have asked the *patrón* to give us more benefits: pieces of land to farm, and help when we needed it—money or whatever—in case someone ran out of capital to work with and needed a loan, because that would increase production. Yes, I believe that now that can be done. Before, with the *patrón,* I don't know.

I think that the best thing for my sons is to stay in agriculture. Of course they could be workers or employees in the city; it is good work but I think it's better to stay here in the country, because one lives easier here. There's more to eat, and more room. In the city if you don't have money you can't do anything about it, but in the *campo* all you have to do is take a walk to your neighbor's house and they'll give you a little bit of food to eat, and you can get through the day like that. Work in the country is more secure, and it's better to have security—even if you have to obey orders—than to be more free, as you say, in the city.

What do I think about the people of Culiprán? Well, now that they have the land they feel good—better than in other *fundos,* naturally. They say that they're more at ease now. Who knows if the others envy them? Maybe so, but nobody says anything about it.

As for me, the *patrón* was always very good to me because we were brought up together. He's always given me all my food, and everything I have I owe to him. Why should I say anything bad about him? If some people rebelled it must be because they have something wrong with them, no? Or they don't think, or don't work and just want to take it easy. Of course, not everyone can live just the same, because we're not all equal, right? If there are so many other people of my age, why haven't they risen on the scale, too? I believe it's because they have a different way of thinking [*moral de pensar*]. They don't have to be loafers or gamblers or drunks. They have had the same opportunities I had but they haven't been able to be more than I am. If I've got some savings it's because I've been more economical. And I had kids who were better adjusted to the things of life. They didn't get mixed up in this business of taking the land.

How were things here before? No matter how many others have told you—I don't know if they're in agreement with me or are just stupid—I'm telling you the truth. Things here with *patrón* Marín were just as they were supposed to be, no more. You worked, as you were supposed to, and as they do everywhere on all the *fundos.* And it wasn't only on Culiprán that one went to work early and quit late—on all the rural haciendas it's the same. And the pay, too. What it was supposed to be, no more. About what the law says. *Regalías:* you could go and get firewood—whatever you wanted for yourself. Right here I can show you the stack of wood I have. Of course the lazy ones, who don't think like that, just wander around.

You want to know what I think about what's going on here now? I'm sixty years old and it's the same for me as it is for a child. If a man retires and they say that they're going to kick him out, then why won't they do that to me? Of course it's not that serious with me; not because I've still got some breath left in me, but because I'm working with the real *patrón*. Don't you see that he has his animals here? It's up to him to accept the agrarian reform by the first of April. After that I don't know what will happen. I might stay and work or I might go with them, but at my age I can't work alongside young men. What I'll do is I'll put my son to work, and I'll stay around and do something here—even if it's just sweeping the house [laughs].

I can go to Melipilla to buy what we need. We always buy wholesale there, but you also have to buy things from the salesmen who come out here if you need something in a hurry. But it's cheaper in Melipilla. You can figure it out for yourself: if you buy in town, won't it be cheaper than from somebody who sells in the countryside?

You ask if people—agitators—ever came here to the *fundo?* They sure have, it's been like that all my life [laughs], and they stir things up, and I can't say that's good. Why should I like it if they come to insist that I join the union. If I'm a Christian Democrat, how am I going to be a Socialist or a Communist? And they come up and demand that I sign the Communist membership book. How can I be a Communist if I belong to the Christian Democratic party and I was a Conservative before that. I was with the Conservatives and then I switched to the Democrats. Why can't I be a Democrat, then. All my life I have voted for the Conservatives. All my life I have been a Christian—since I came of age—and I'm going to be sixty this year. I was born in 1907 and after I came of age I served in the military, too. Yes, sir, all my life with the Conservatives, because I saw that, if one doesn't live with the people who have money, well, who are you going to live with? You have to live with the right ones.

We were all born in this house. My grandfather built it and he died when he was ninety-five years old. So we've had this house for more than one hundred years, and do you know why? Because we've gotten along well with the people who have owned the *fundo*. The *patrones* before gave us land. They thought well of my grandfather, and of my father after him. So we've always led an honorable, good life. If we had been lazy or had a black sheep in the family, or if we hadn't been well brought up everything would have been different.

Some people think that the *fundo* doesn't need a *patrón* to run it. Well, everything has to change just like Chile itself is changing and our children work for us now, but I don't think that they know how different we are from them. Their way of living—this "modern" way of living—is different. There is another way to live.

The best way to run a *fundo*—you want to know what I think? Well, you should have seen the *fundo* when it was irrigated. Now it's all dry. There are no gates to the pastures. How can it be better? When the animals walk out into the road it's dangerous for everyone because someday they could kill some people. Why wasn't it like that before? Because now the people have rebelled. I'm not a Communist or a Socialist, and if the Conservative party dies I'll have to go with the Democrats. I voted for Frei and Don Jorge Alessandri and I'm not afraid to tell anyone, anywhere, and with honor. By now the people will have told you something depending on whether or not they're rebels, but my opinion is that things are not the same as they used to be. You want to know what has changed, but if I tell you all that, we might be in danger—they're capable of coming to kill me. No, sir, I'm no stool pigeon [laughs]. They could come here to kill me. So my opinion is just that one doesn't live as well as before. I think that the people have lost their respect. There, I have told you everything and I'm not going to tell you anything else [laughs].

How do I notice that they've lost respect? I'll tell you the truth—the truth from a man of sixty who's been around since 1907. In some things you can't help but notice that they've lost respect. In one thing: in this "modern" way of living where everything has to change, and the political ideas, too. Do I think that things have to change or if they were better before? I can tell you that before—after the insurance came out—you paid a five, one centavo for the insurance, and you were insured on the spot. But it was different then; now everything has to change.

And my sons, not one of them has taken part in this movement or joined the union, either, because I am still boss around here. They listen to me and when they go out around here they just watch the others from a distance because if the others see them they chase my boys off. One day a leader chased them away. They were mad and it's not fair because they have a right to listen to what they want. But since the others were the owners of the *fundo*, you see . . .

If they were badly off here on the *fundo*, of course they'd get desperate, if the conditions on the *fundo* were bad. But that's ridiculous. I have to say that it's ridiculous, because although it's true that they took advantage of us in signing up for the social laws, and that there wasn't enough pasture for the animals and things like that—even so, it wasn't much. Later, though, that was all fixed and we had it easier. It's true that the *patrón* was to blame for some of it, but after it was fixed things were different. But they were already asking for the expropriation of the *fundo* and didn't even want to make any deals.

Did the *patrón* have any defects? I didn't think he had any. He was a man of the law—except for a few little things—to those he liked—to those he didn't like, no. On the other *fundos*, like San Manuel, they have pretty houses with radios and cooperatives, but the people were never the same as the people here. The people here were rolling in money because there was more money around here where the people made their regular salary. They made the salary they should make and nobody tried to fool them with a piece of candy or something else. It's not that they earned more than in San Manuel, but the land produces more here.

If you want to know my opinion about how to make it easier to work the land, now that there is *asentamiento,* just give me three cuadras and I'll start to work them tomorrow. I'll work them myself, independently, because when everyone works together you're never going to make money. If you were a farmer and knew how we farm here, you'd understand. Because if I have a *peón,*—a good *peón*—none of these people who have *asentamiento* and are all wet behind the ears are going to work as well. If I've got the means to work with, how are they going to make as much as I do? I used to have a cuadra of the best land wherever I asked for it. And then I sold the produce in the capital. A year ago this month I sold two truckloads of potatoes in Santiago. I paid one thousand pesos a sack for freight and sold two hundred sacks in February. That's why I agreed with the *patrón* about the *regalías.* Even if there are others who don't have as much—who haven't risen as high—because you know that everyone has his place on the ladder. Not everyone can be the same on a *fundo.* There are privates, corporals, a sergeant, and then the colonels and so forth.

You ask if the taking of the *fundo* and the *asentamiento* has had an effect on the people around here—if it has encouraged them. Well, in some other places not half of the people want this—not even a few. When they see what's happening in Santa Inés and here in Culiprán, half of the people are turning back because they see that the social laws are bad [social security is not paid]. They can't get their personal documents brought up to date. Family men have gone without their documents and the hospitals won't take them. Sure, that has happened here, too. I heard one man who was complaining a lot because they wouldn't fix his papers. They have to be in order so that the family allowance can be paid. The *patrón* used to take care of that, but if everyone is *patrón,* what with the *asentamiento,* will it be the same? All this and a bunch of inexperienced kids who sharecrop just to pass their time—how can it be the same? It can't be. It's better to have one *patrón*—as long as he's a good one. As far as the social laws are concerned, the president of the Republic should take care of them. Let him take care of our laws. To my way of thinking, that's worth more than giving us lands to sharecrop. Maybe you think something else; the others can think whatever they like, but I preferred it like it was, and many of those you have talked to think the same. At least they've all told you similar things, haven't they? You want to know if the people are happy, don't you? Listen, what I'm going to tell you is mean, but the no-account people here are the ones who might be happy. The worthwhile, solid people can't be. Why did they prefer to have lights in the houses before? And why don't they have light now? They wanted their houses to have slate roofs—not thatch—but what have they got now? But no one complains now. Before, the *patrón* had to fix up their kitchens and roof their houses, and why don't they complain now? It was better to have a *patrón*. But, you see how it is here now. What else can you think? It doesn't matter to a man who's used to sleeping on the floor or being bit by fleas, but it makes the nights very long for one who is used to a different kind of life. Sure, there are lazy people, but I think it's more a lack of brains than of work. That's what I'd say—just a lack of brains. They want everything on a platter here.

The women also had a hand in it. Yes, I think they had influence. But I can tell you one thing: the land there is the same as it is here, and my wife has a garden with onions and other vegetables, and the other women come to buy onions and chiles and tomatoes. Why don't they raise them themselves?

My wife is married to a clever man and spends her time planting and preparing vegetables and greens. What I want to know is why the other women don't do that. They wouldn't have to come and buy from us then, and they all come. There's one man retired from the army who was amazed. He grabbed his head with his hands like this and asked me why my *señora* does this work and why the others don't, since the lands are the same. Don't you see that it has to do with your way of thinking?

And why do they have to be Communists? This man came here, with the other . . . what is his name? The ones who led the people, and they told them, "We won the hardest fight—to expropriate the *fundo*—but now we have another fight with the CORA because they're just a bunch of oafs." That's what the man said to them. It's not good for me to be telling you this, because I don't want to get into politics and someday they're going to find out that I was giving you this explanation. But how can I be happy with this when I never fought for it? I am a Democrat, and if I voted for Frei and for Don Jorge Alessandri before him, and for Carlos Ibáñez del Campo before him, it was for a reason, no? I've never failed to vote in my life. And I've given the sixteen or twenty-five votes from my family to the right. You ask me why? Because it's the most orderly and peaceful way to live. You get along better with the *patrones* who like you. So the future is easier for you—especially if you're a married man.

The majority here voted for Allende in the last election,[1] and we put up a tremendous fight. We don't know the man who is *jefe* of the committee

[1] The 1964 presidential election.

now—he's new. It's not that he's not an orderly person himself—it's that they can't get themselves in order. It's because they haven't quit fighting, that's all. You can see it: right now they want to turn him out and vote on a new *jefe*. Yesterday they had a meeting. They have a meeting every week and that's what I can't understand. It's worse than a dogfight. There is no discipline, it's just foolishness. They aren't interested in telling each other things—they don't want to talk about anything. They don't respect this *jefe*, because they don't respect anyone. They got rid of the other *jefe*[2] because he punched a man who was running the threshing machine. He hit him because he had his wine jug with him—drinking at his job. The CORA people are high-class gentlemen, it's true, but they know their way around here. They are involved in everything and know the *campo*. This man Jesús, he knows a lot. There's nothing bad to say about him, and even though I don't know him well, I find that he knows a lot. But they don't have anyone to impose respect: they need the *patrón* or some tough character to tell them to cut out the tricks and get things in order. Because if the *fundo* isn't expropriated by the government and if the *inquilinos* have taken it without paying for it, well, what else can you do. The Corporation has to impose itself—a real *jefe* has to come along. That's what has to be done. Maybe it's because they have political *fueros* [payoffs].

You ask what my aspirations are for my children. Well, I'd like the women to be seamstresses and live in their own homes and not go out to work around here, or hang around in the *boliches* [cabarets]. Why should they go around saying, "Long live the Socialists, long live the Communists." The men from CORA have heard that sort of thing right here. There's no reason for them to collect information when they get the best data right here.

For my sons, agriculture is best. It's better because you get the money all at once [laughs]. I've always worked on this *fundo*. I was born here in this house that my grandfather built when he got married. You can see it's just the house of a typical Chilean *roto*. Now they want everything without working: let's go to the dance, let's take a walk. Just let everything fall apart, and if there's a place to play cards, let's play cards.

I don't understand just what you're asking me about the future of this country, but I think that we live more peacefully here, and that it's one of the best countries there is in the whole world. I listen to the news on the radio every morning, at one o'clock, and every night. I know about everything that's going on in the country and in Europe. That's why I think Chile is one of the best countries in the world.

[2] A CORA official.

I'm resigned to the way politics are, but I'm not for the unions. Don't even mention them to me [laughs]. I can't even stand to think about them. A union, at my age? What do I need an agrarian union for—now that the *patrón* is gone? What are they for if not to fight with the *patrón* for the social laws? I didn't even want a union when we had a *patrón,* because he and I got along. How could I go against my *patrón* when I was on good terms with him and he gave me all the privileges: pasture for the animals, and milk cows. How could I go against him? I'm not saying that the others don't have the right to form a union. I'm not unreasonable. If they didn't get along with the *patrón,* then I can almost say that they have a right. People came from outside to organize them. They came from Melipilla and Santiago, and if they hadn't come, do you think they would have dared? No. It was the Socialists and the Communists who won here. Señor Altamirano came from the Socialists and others came, too. If they hadn't come they would never have beaten the *patrón.* On the contrary, the *patrón* would have beaten them because it was a real fight and they were getting weaker. The *patrón* had them cowed and the people stopped listening to them here in Melipilla. They had to go to Santiago. They fought hard there and if it weren't for the Socialists and Communists they wouldn't have gotten anything. That's why they don't like the Christian Democrats and say that they've sold out. They nearly said that right to the faces of Señor Alwyn[3] and the Mayor of Melipilla. That's why I can't tell you anymore. And how can I think that is good, when I was never with them?

Oh no, I never confronted them. We defended *patrón* Marín while it was our duty to take care of him, but afterward they took the *fundo* and didn't allow us to. And how could just a few of us defend ourselves? Could 20 of us take care of 150? They had sickles and forked poles and I don't know what else. They didn't even let the administrator go into the mill. When the authorities came from Melipilla, they wouldn't let them, either. Not the lieutenant, not anybody. They didn't obey anyone. No, I'm not saying that the *patrón* was completely blameless in this. Especially when he wanted to take away the pasturage for the animals. But that was worked out later and they didn't want to obey then, either. And they never obeyed him again. They asked for bigger salaries and the government's social laws.

[3] A Christian Democrat senator.

C. Interview with a Follower

The *patrón* we had here was the worst possible. He didn't fulfill his obligations to us. He only gave us a cuarto of land as *regalía,* and, since I was a master carpenter, I had a right to one and a half cuartos. But he only gave me one. So here I was working just one cuarto and making a tiny salary. We made 8,000 or 9,000 at most. Every month we got 7,500 pesos. We started to complain one time when Don Eduardo [Marín] held the money back because of something to do with the animals we had. That was when we got some life in us and began to protest. We called a strike here—we didn't want to work. So all that money that he'd been keeping from us was given back: some got 9,000 pesos, others 12,000. Later he divided it equally according to the number of animals we had. He had to give all that money back.

Don Manuel Muñoz was the one who organized that movement. He's from Santiago, from Puente Alto. When could we have done it alone? Never. *Compañeros* from the Socialist party came from Melipilla later. They are the ones who've done everything here. What could we have done? The only thing we could do was appeal to Santiago. Of course we could have stopped the *patron* with just our own people because we were united. There were enough of us here for that—two hundred and seventy or eighty.

The only *regalía* that *señor* Marín gave us was this cuarto of land. He didn't give us anything. Not all of the *patrones* are like that—there are better ones, much better ones. But in his case the situation couldn't go on. Never. If you went to ask him for a favor, or if you asked for a loan of some cash when you had a sick child, he would say, "How can I loan you the money if I don't have any?" That would be his answer. Then he'd turn his pockets inside out to show that he didn't have anything. Once the *inquilinos* gave him a piece of biscuit to eat, the kind that is made here on the *fundo,* and he ate it even though it was four days old and stale. If he hadn't been like that, the people wouldn't have wanted to take over the *fundo.* Nothing would have happened, because, if the *patrón* had treated the *inquilinos* well, we wouldn't have done anything. I don't know what it will be like without a *patrón*, but judging from the way things are now, it's not bad. It is better this way because each one works for himself in the community. Everyone here is eager to work. You wonder if maybe it's better to have a *patrón?* Well, if it means having *mayordomos* and *empleados* ordering you around, then I think it's much better this way, because we already know how to work hard in order to have a little more afterward. It is better to work for yourself than for a *patrón.* That's how I'd prefer it. And I think you make more money, too, and without trouble.

I don't know how the question of the insurance is going to come out. They say they're going to keep our papers up to date . . . maybe so. The unions are only half organized, in my opinion. Of course it's good that there is a union, but I don't really know how it is or if it has advantages.

Before when we wanted to talk with the *patrón* we couldn't because you never saw him around here. We had to talk with the administrator—he was like the *patrón* for us. Naturally you can't go alone when you want to have things changed. Everyone has to be together, like we are here.

You ask if the takeover on Culiprán has influenced the neighboring *fundos?* Yes. For example, they've become enthusiastic. Look, there goes Polanco and the five leaders—the aristocracy [laughs]. Of course all the neighbor *fundos* have been organized by this *fundo.* There is a committee, but in Popeta it's not too large. The *fundo* is expropriated but the thing still hasn't been resolved like it has here. They are organized. I don't know the leaders, but I do know some of the people. I know several *campesinos,* but only by sight. Still, I think there are too few in Popeta to do the same thing we did here. I don't know about the other *fundos.* There are about sixty on Popeta, but I don't know how many are on the other *fundos,* and they change, too.

Another thing that was important here was that people came from Santiago and we were all united. But if they have a good *patrón* they shouldn't do it. It's only right to do it to the bad *patrones,* but there are *patrones* who are good to the *inquilinos.* They give them all kinds of *regalías,* so that all the workers do is screw the *patrón,* that's all. No, I don't think I would help them. And if the *patrón* is good to them then it's unjust, and they shouldn't try to bother him.

Look, here come the men from CORA. There's Don Lucho who's in charge of the *fundo* along with Don Jesús.

You want to know if I think that now that we have this organization the *campesinos* can put things in order and work the *fundo* better than before? I am better off now, although who knows how things will turn out. Anyway, the small farms [*chacras*] are working better now. There are more farms being cultivated because more effort has been made this year. And before hardly anyone planted wheat—or only two little fields just for the use of the *fundo.*

Do I prefer it here, or would I rather go to San Manuel? I live here . . . How could I leave now? Even if they offered to take me over there with a good salary and *regalías,* I wouldn't go. I'd only go if they ran us out of here. But I don't want to—I don't like it there. How could I move when I've been born and raised here. I'm fifty-six years old and was born here. Sure, I was away from the *fundo* for about fifteen years when I was single. I was in Mandinga; I lived there and in Melipilla. I lived in Santaigo and Maipú, then I came back here again.

What would we have done if the *carabineros* had tried to stop us with their guns when we took over the *fundo?* Well, we would have killed some *carabineros.* We wouldn't have gone back. When the major of *carabineros* got his courage and came up threatening to put me away if we tried to stop him, I told him that if he came in he would lose his head. I told him to keep out. All of us armed ourselves and got ready, and did they come in? They didn't even touch the gates to try to open them because they were scared. So the whole thing was over right there. We had confidence because we were all united. And we felt that everyone supported us because senators and deputies had come from Santiago. There were plenty of leaders from Santiago to protect us. The women and girls were with us, too, and we were here for ten or twelve days.

I don't leave the *fundo* much. I don't have any relatives in the other *fundos* around here. Once in a while I go to Melipilla when I have to. I don't belong to the committee—I belong to the Committee of May. I do belong to the union, though, and I go to meetings whenever there is one—every week. When there is a meeting they talk. They have to say something.

You ask if the *campesinos* from anywhere in the department of Melipilla could do what we've done. I don't think so, because they wouldn't be united. If they are united, I don't see it. The leaders here are good because everyone is united—all the *compañeros* are together.

I haven't gotten into politics. I want my kids to keep working here. My married daughters are working now, but I've still got three little girls here at home who haven't started working at anything yet.

I didn't belong to that football club they used to have and I didn't go to the games. I leave the *fundo* once or twice a month. I buy what we need in Melipilla or Santiago; I never buy from the salesmen who come to the *fundo.* Never.

Yes, when Marín was *patrón,* there were some people here who had more than others. And there are still some who aren't in this with us—we call them *amarillos* [yellow]. They've never pulled their own weight; they've never gone along with us. They don't join the union; they don't pay dues; they don't even give a little help; they don't do anything. But what can we do about it? They're owners, aren't they? Yes, those *amarillos* are popping up all over. They were the *empleados* before the takeover.

Do I think it's better to work the land in community rather than each one working his own piece? Not in community, no. I think we'd all end up fighting. I'd rather have them give us each a piece of land. Sure, I'd have to get some help: I'd need seed, but I have two teams of animals, a plow, and all the other necessities. And of course I have work hands—my own sons would help me and there are three of them here.

We have planted this year and we have one cuadra or a little more. We have a half cuadra that we got as a *regalía* through the union. Before, when we had one cuarto, we couldn't sell enough to pay the expenses because we had to put aside enough seed for the next year and for our use at home. We had to put all that aside and it left nothing to sell—eight or ten sacks sometimes. But you couldn't sell more off the cuarto because you had to put the whole thing in potatoes. So that with one cuarto you didn't even make enough to buy clothes. Seven sacks from one cuarto was all we could make . . . and with so many kids.

D. Interview with a Present Leader of the Peasant Committee

[Before being elected leader he was an ordinary *inquilino* on the *fundo*. He is thirty-five years old.]

The problems we had here were due to something that the *patrón* himself always told us. When he came he said that there was a raise in the minimum wage since the first of May. He always paid us at the end of the month—the last Saturday of the month. But he didn't warn us at all about the cuts he was thinking of making. Then he called us to be paid at night on the sixth of June, and he didn't say anything about it then either, but he had made tremendous cuts: nine thousand for pasturing our animals, three thousand a year for the use of his carts, and he took six hundred pesos per month for bread and charged for water. He was about to take off for our tools, too.

Those who work as day laborers [*voluntarios*] and only work six or seven days a month came out owing him money. They didn't make enough to pay and had to try to pay him the next month. That was when we said to ourselves, "We can't allow this."

We went to tell a councilman of the Christian Democratic party, Don Jorge González. It was Monday, and that same day we struck. The councilman came early and took me to the town hall in Melipilla where the mayor was ready to make a deal with us, and we signed a formal agreement [*acta de avenimiento*] that was only a demand that the *patrón* pay the *inquilinos* 2,450 and the migrants 2,700 without taking anything out for insurance, which he would pay for himself. When the next payday came he was still making the same cuts. He took off 290 pesos a day under the new salary. So we struck again. Then the mayor told us that the cuts had to be made—even after he'd signed the paper and told us that it couldn't be done. The mayor, the labor inspector, the Melipilla judge, and even Don Alberto González, the councilman, told us that these withholdings had to stand. We said they couldn't keep the money and we decided to go on strike.

So we reported to Santiago and to the councilman of the Socialist party, as well. We told Matías Núñez and Pedro Martínez Romo. Matías Núñez immediately got the director of the Peasant Federation, Manuel Muñoz, on the phone, and he came and established our union and wrote up a legal petition for us. From there we went on with the fight. The owner also wanted to take away the land that he'd given us before. He wanted to take half a cuarto away from us and rent us the other half at ten thousand per month. We wouldn't buy that and went to see the vice-president of the Corporation [CORA], Don Rafael Moreno. We asked for the expropriation of the *fundo* because it wasn't being well used and the *patrón* didn't want to give us anything. The papers authorizing the change were signed on 15 July. Councilmen and deputies came and we had a party that night. We had to stick to our intention, though, because the *patrón* wanted to give us a bit of land if we'd sign a paper for it. We didn't want that. The mayor wanted us to sign; so did the inspector and the judge and the councilman A. González of the Christian Democrats. But we kept saying no, and we never signed. Thanks to that the Corporation took charge of the *fundo*. Now we work as partners with the CORA and run the *fundo* ourselves with a representative of the Corporation, Don Mario García. Today there is going to be a meeting with him because he wants to discuss some problems with us—seriously.

It's only a rumor, but I've heard that they want the foreman [*capataz*] and the rest of the *empleados* to stay on. They say the CORA wants to keep them on as *empleados*. We don't have to allow that under any circumstances. We have fought for this land and we want people who work on the *fundo*. We don't want to be pushed by anyone. We're used to working and running the *fundo* ourselves now, so we're not going to accept that. I think that if the problem comes up I'm going to ask for an interview with the vice-president of the Corporation or with the president himself—Don Hugo Trivelli.

I was an *inquilino* here. My father was an *inquilino* on this *fundo*, too, and he was already here when Marín bought it. I know that he bought it for 5,730,000 pesos and paid 2 million on the mortgage. So he bought it for 7,730,000 pesos in all. We read in the newspapers that the CORA paid him 2,560,000 for the *fundo*—10 percent in cash and the rest paid out over twenty-five years.

I was born very close to here—eighteen kilometers away, but I was brought here when I was two. The lands of Culiprán are the only ones I recognize. I've never left here to go anywhere except when I was in the service and was stationed in the Andes back in 1943. I have no relatives [outside his immediate family] here on the *fundo*, but I have cousins in Villa Alhué and other relatives in Melipilla. I don't go to Melipilla much. In the last few months I've gone twice to take care of complaints, and sometimes I go to take care of family business like getting medicine. You also have to go to town to see the doctor. I'm single and my mother is alive; I keep the house with my other brothers, who are bachelors too.

I didn't belong to any political party, and, as I said to the others, we have to fight for our own well-being even without the political parties. It's true that several times we went to Melipilla to ask for the help and cooperation of the parties, but our problem was our own private fight; it was for the welfare of our homes and families and all those who live on the *fundo*. That is why we don't allow any outsiders to come in, but just work with those who are here. We asked for the expropriation of the *fundo* for the people who are working it—those of us who were exploited by the *patrón* and don't want to go on being exploited. That's why I'm against the problem that Señor García is trying to stir up.

There was no organization here before. The people just worked, and when the *patrón* committed an abuse we would meet and complain for our own good. There was a sports club but I didn't belong to it, although I cooperated with them because I like to help in everything that has to do with the entertainment and well-being of the people on the *fundo*. There was no cooperative, but I've heard from the people who've been here longest that there was a cooperative of 280 people here before. All the people of the *fundo* had deposited a little cash, and it was their cooperative. Then Señor Marín took it from them. He robbed them and took everything to the *fundo* of Huachún Bajo.[1] It was robbery.

After that the people bought from a store that he set up on the *fundo*. He let them buy with chits [*vales*] that he gave them. So you bought the things you needed and paid with the days you worked. You had to pay just like with any salesman. But that ended over thirty years ago, and then the people bought from private salesmen whenever they came with things from town. They bought things however they could.

Most people here have radios. We don't, and haven't thought of buying one. We do read newspapers when we have them brought from town or when we go ourselves and buy them.

At first the administrator made it easier for some people—those whom he wanted to help. Some had tools or horses, or more land, and he made it easier for them to work more land. He said that whoever knew how to work would work. But lately he didn't want to give land because he didn't want the people to farm it. Everyone here has his own team. Right now I have two teams—they're horses that we've been raising here because they haven't bought any colts. We've kept the colts from a mare that belonged

---

[1] Another *fundo* owned by Marín.

to my father. We've been increasing our animals since then, and we're not finished yet.

There are some *inquilinos* who are richer than others because the *fundo* gave them privileges and the administrator helped them buy what they needed. Most of them are *empleados,* but there are a few *inquilinos,* too—but very few. And now the *empleados* stay on at the *fundo* and they're the ones who don't want to work in community with us. I think they've gone to the Corporation and the CORA is going to let them stay on as *empleados.* That is what we're not going to allow. That's why I want to talk with the *compañeros* before going to the meeting: in order to come to an agreement with the *compañeros* of the committee on this point.

Before the Comité del Asentamiento each worker took care of himself; each man worked for himself and the work wasn't done in common. They only worked as much as they had to and if they made some money they paid other *compañeros* to do the work. If there was some trouble with Señor Marín each one worked it out individually and the people didn't band together. If they did, he threw them and all their things out in the street. That's why he threw some people out in 1940, for example.

I find that one lives more peacefully with the houses separated. Before, the houses on this *fundo* were completely separated because when Marín bought the land there were more than two hundred houses. But he ended that. He'd chase a man off and tear down his house. He tore down something like one hundred houses that way because the authorities would let him do anything he wanted. Not many people came from outside, because there wasn't much work. Two animals and not many *regalías.* He paid us by the day and gave us a little plot of land. He didn't give us anything.

No, I don't believe that all *patrones* think the same as he did. Not all the *patrones* are bad. The bad owners are very few. On the adjoining *fundos*—San Manuel, for instance—the *patrones* are more humanitarian with the people. They sell them things on easy terms and the people pay little by little out of their salaries. If we had lived under conditions like those of San Manuel, we wouldn't have asked CORA to expropriate the *fundo* and give it to the *inquilinos.* We wouldn't have done anything, because when Señor Marín was making trouble for us here, the *patrón* of San Manuel called his people together and raised their salaries a little and raised the *regalías,* so the people kept right on working happily. If there's a good humanitarian *patrón,* then it's better to stay at home with your *regalías* and with that *patrón* than to work in community. One lives more peacefully and there are more guarantees, and the people are well treated.

Is there any risk in working for ourselves? No. Because everyone is working for himself and each one has to work on his own, and you always put everything into your work when you know you're working your own land.

If we made this *fundo* pay before, when it all went to Señor Marín, then why shouldn't we make it pay now that it's going to be for us? It would be ideal if—after the two or three years of reform that the CORA proposes— we could work the *fundo* collectively. That's preferable because everyone helps everyone else.

Well, I can tell you that we want to be an example to the other *campesinos* from other *fundos* around here. We know that all the *campesinos* are watching us and are going to follow our example—all those who have bad *patrones* like we had here. And if they don't have the courage, or if they need help, we can cooperate with them, especially if they have bad *patrones*. Now I believe that the *campesino* has to be organized because unity is the only strength the *campesino* has. He has no other strength. The unions are very important in the *fundo* because they are the worker's only defense. The political parties are also important, of course, because the help of the Congress comes through them. They helped us here and we have thanked the congressmen of the Socialist party, the Communist party, and also some from the Christian Democratic party.

If, as you say this has happened in other places, the landowners want to organize to defend themselves by force, then the *campesinos* have to stay united and strengthen themselves. That is, they have to be ready for whatever comes. They have to be ready to lay down their lives; if one loses his life, it's gone, but is lost for the good of his people. Of course there comes a time when each *campesino* has to defend himself alone; but you always have to ask for help from Congress, because if the congressmen aren't on your side you're lost. We, for example, obeyed Senator Altamirano.

Like you say, I think that the agrarian reform should eliminate all the agricultural landowners and divide the land among the *campesinos* so that they can work in peace and produce for the country. It has to be that way because the bad *patrones* monopolize the land, like Señor Marín, and mess up the countryside and everyone in it.

I am the leader of the union and vice-president of the Peasant Committee. My job is to represent the president of the Committee when he is gone. The election was held this November. First they elected the heads of families and they in turn elected us by secret ballot—with a ballot box. Everything still doesn't function well in our offices, because we're just getting started, but up to now we haven't had any trouble with the members of the Peasant Committee. No serious problems. But from now on I think we are going to have problems because of this question of the *empleados*. And many problems are going to arise after that. We're going to have to be prepared to tell the Corporation not to put any more *inquilinos* on the *fundo* with us, and not to interrupt our work. Some people—*jefes* and the like—come in from other places. We have to accept that because it's done by agreements [*escrituras*] so that there's nothing anybody can do. And since the *escrituras* are the law, we are all in agreement. All of us are united and we know we have rights.

E. Interview with a *Campesino* Who Favored the Takeover

[An *inquilino* like the rest, he also ran a small store where the other *inquilinos* gathered to talk. He is fifty years old.]

Politics came to a stop here many years ago during the time of Pedro Aguirre Cerda. There was a revolution on the *fundo* and they let us stay provided we didn't get involved in politics again. At that time—in 1940 and 1941—the Socialist party was organized here, and since then the *compañeros* have kept the idea—the fighting idea—of taking advantage of the right time to seize the land. We always have had the intention of finding a better life—of living a little easier. Pedro Aguirre Cerda was the presidential candidate of the Socialist party. How many of us were there? Some 150 or less. The whole *fundo* was involved—it was the "product" of the Socialists. When the party was organized we began to go out to Santiago, San Antonio, and Noviciado to make propaganda for Don Pedro. We went to several places. I was head of the militia because all the Socialist parties had militias. It was a separate group that had to keep order in case there was some trouble.

In Melipilla they were afraid to make propaganda because there were many rightists, so the peasant *compañeros* came to us. Isn't that funny? That's right, in Melipilla they were so few they didn't count for anything, but here on the *fundo* we got three truckloads of men together. When we got to Melipilla they had everything for us from rubber stamps to those clubs the cops use. We divided up: one stood guard, others painted slogans, and others put up posters. They came to find us one night because all the rightist propaganda was ready and they were afraid to put up the propaganda of Don Pedro. At dawn we were in the town. It was just getting light when we left, and the whole town, the plaza, and all the major streets were covered with slogans and propaganda.

It was then that the Socialist party was organized here on the *fundo,* and three *compañeros* were kicked out. The *patrón* booted them out because they didn't want to get out of the party. The *patrón* gave them that advice and offered them 1,001 things to get them to leave the party but they wouldn't, so he came and threw them out. And my father-in-law was one of those who got the axe. I was living with him, and I arrived at just the right time—when they were moving his things out—and said to the administrator: "Señor, I wasn't told anything. Ask them not to throw my things in the street." Then he told me that he'd taken my things out because he was kicking me out, too. So I looked for another place. I went to a compadre's place and stayed with him. That very afternoon I came back and moved my stuff over there and I stayed with my compadre for a year. Yes, the *patrón* threw them out; he fired two here, and he fired others in [Culiprán] Bajo. They just had to leave, that's all, because he kicked them all out.

What happened then? What's happened up to now? Well, there was the change of presidents, and we began to take heart when Señor Eduardo Frei was elected. We said, "Now Señor Frei has to help, he has to help us." In those days the leaders of the Socialist party didn't come around anymore. The only ones who came were from the Christian Democrats and the Communist party. And they also came around to campaign for the election of deputies and senators. So we were encouraged again and we said, "Now we have to organize ourselves again." We voted for Frei even though we were Socialists because his was the party that could help us. And something else happened too—I'll tell it to you straight. All of us were for Allende. Everyone—the whole *fundo*—was Allendista and then a candidate for deputy, Caupolicán Peña, came out here and blew it all. He told us that the rich people bought us off for a piece of bread, that they treated us like dogs—throwing us a piece of meat or giving us a sandwich. He said that if we didn't vote with him we had sold ourselves. So you see, the next day everyone had changed their minds. If it weren't for that everyone would be for Allende here. It was that gentleman who made the campaign fail here. But many people still voted for *compañero* Allende. The ladies voted too. There are 200 voters here and 150 voted. In other places they have twice that many.

Yes, sure it's true that some of the women go to the other side. They're more rebellious and many times they get fooled. It was because they were afraid: like when the Christian Democrats said that if Allende were elected their children would be taken away from them. That frightened the women, and they voted for Frei so that nobody would take their babies. That's the truth. Did we believe it? Sure, some believed it. We men didn't, but the women did—they're weaker. Did we talk about politics? Yes and no. Some people who are more prepared talk about it, but you know that sometimes the rest of us don't understand those things.

F. Interview with a Local Political Leader

[This man acted as a contact between the *campesinos* of the *fundo* and the political organizations of the town.]

I want to make it clear that in 1963 the Christian Democratic party campaigned heavily and only elected one councilman. The Communist party was also around and they didn't even get one. On the other hand, the Socialist party elected two councilmen and the votes came from the *fundo*. But after the parliamentary election they were all with the Socialist party. That was when this fellow Caupolicán Peña came, because unfortunately the Socialist party had no deputy in the fourth district, and we were supporting him. He was the one who expressed himself badly and it seemed to them . . . well, the peasant *compañeros* know how to read, too, and, after all, they have their pride and personality, too, and they were treated a bit brusquely—like the *compañero* here said—about the peasants selling themselves for a piece of bread or a swallow of wine or piece of meat. So that many of those who might have voted for that man voted for the Christian Democrat candidates.

Coming back to the takeover. The first thing that was done here was the formal list of demands (*pliego de peticiones*) when we were being directed and supported by the Christian Democrats through the councilman from Melipilla, Alberto González. And they suggested a march to Melipilla to put pressure on the owner so that he'd comply with our petition. But the Christian Democrats' list of demands was badly written. The inspector of labor in Melipilla accepted it but it wasn't good, because, among other things, it asked for an eight-hour workday when that's been a law for many years, and if it's the law you don't have to ask for it. But they didn't comply with it anyway.

Even though the Christian Democrats have the mayor and the inspector of labor in their pockets, and all the authorities depend on the present government, justice wasn't done. So the people turned to the Socialist party, because, when we made that march from the hacienda to Melipilla with the leaders of the Christian Democrats, they just told the *campesinos* to go and that in Melipilla the councilmen of the Socialist party would join the march because it was a joint project. But that was a lie because they didn't invite us—the leaders of the Socialist party—or even tell us anything about it. When they failed and realized that the *campesinos* of the hacienda Culiprán had been put off several times by the Christian Democrats, then *compañero* Muñoz Bahamondes of the Federación Campesina e Indígena came in here and worked up a new list of demands. The inspector of labor in Melipilla refused to receive it because there was already an earlier one. But this new petition was signed by all the *inquilinos*—more than two hundred signatures—and Muñoz Bahamondes and the leaders demanded that they accept it.

When they accepted it we saw that we wouldn't get anything out of the inspector of labor and we had to go to the Board of Conciliation, the criminal judge, and the Municipal Court (there is no labor judge, so the Municipal Court judge serves as the labor judge). We got into a lot of red tape there, too. Sometimes the *patrón* didn't attend and when he did we couldn't come to any agreement with him. There were many days between sessions, and the last session was set for 28 October, when the *compañeros* should have already had the land to begin working it. Time was passing, and so in the petition all that we asked for was a half cuadra for everyone instead of the fourth he was offering us. That was the "quid" in the affair. One hundred and eleven asked for one half cuadra—that's fifty-six cuadras from the eight thousand that the *patrón* owns. That would have solved the problem, but he didn't want to let go of those fifty-six cuadras.

Time kept passing and the *campesinos* were demanding stronger action by the leaders and the party. They traveled to Melipilla to ask us to try any means to resolve the problem. Then one afternoon—I remember it was a Saturday—I was called here by the leaders and I saw the fighting mood of the *campesinos* who were gathered in a general assembly right here in front of this *compañero's* house. I saw that they were ready to take other measures—like seizing the land.

They planned it themselves, and on Sunday the seventeenth of October at ten o'clock at night they locked the gates. They dug in and ran up the strike flags. They cut the telephone lines because one of the plans was to isolate the *fundo* in order to get through til Monday, when their support could arrive. In the morning Melipilla was mobilized and they called Senator Altamirano of the Socialist party. He came out here and talked to the peasant groups of Culiprán and then we went immediately to the *fundo* Huachún to see the *compañeros* there. Compañero Altamirano promised them his help and said he would intervene in our favor with Señor Leighton, the minister of the interior, so that *carabineros* wouldn't be sent, because the first shock unit [of *carabineros*] was already in Melipilla at 10:30 in the morning on the eighteenth. The shock unit was in two micro-buses and had submachine guns and helmets and everything to remove us by force. We knew the attitude of the *compañeros* here on the *fundo*—they were ready to die rather than open the gates. It would have been a massacre; sincerely, it would have been a massacre of the peasant com-rades. When Compañero Altamirano arrived Monday the eighteenth, we went back to Melipilla to see how we could intervene to keep the *carabine-ros* from going to the *fundo,* and right there on the radio of Compañero Altamirano's car we heard Deputy A. Alwyn say, among other things, that they, the government, had to support the rights of property and they had to send the police to get the *campesinos* out. Immediately, Compañero Altamirano went to the radio and asked that deputy how the Christian Democrats and the government could talk about law and justice; because even though it wasn't legal for the *campesinos* to take the land, this landowner had distinguished himself for twenty-five or thirty years by his abuses and lack of respect for every part of the law with the acquiescence of the authorities. Justice had never been done by stopping him before, and because of that they had to take the side of the *campesinos.*

And so on Tuesday the minister of the interior received us—five leaders from Huachún and five from Culiprán—and the minister himself could see that there was not going to be any compromise.

G. Interview with a Peasant Follower of the Movement

I've been here on the *fundo* for some thirty-six years. Before the expropriation there was a sports club and I participated in it, but not everybody did—just those who like football. [soccer]. Sometimes we played at the neighbor *fundos*. Thirty, forty, or as many as fifty people from the *fundo* would go. But I don't leave much now.

Yes, we're better off now, since the takeover of the land. I would have liked it if I'd had a good *patrón* like the one on San Manuel. One lives well there, with *regalías*. But it's better to have a parcel of your own. That way the lazy ones don't make anything, but if you aren't lazy and have a good piece of land you can even work at night. You have to keep working—each one on his own land.

When we took the *fundo*, there were some women with us, but not many, maybe five. They were young women, unmarried, twenty or twenty-five years old. But the next day after we'd taken the *fundo*, the women came in the afternoon. They came because we were at the lower gates—we had slept there—and they came to leave food for their husbands.

We weren't afraid of the *carabineros*. When we came to lock the gates there were six *carabineros* on horseback and in a truck. When we came up, they turned on their lights, so we moved farther that way. Not many of us came, because quite a few left and didn't come back until the next day. I was one of the sentinels. There were thirty of us, more or less, so when they told us that they wouldn't let us lock the gates, I took my men and we all went forward and began to lock them. We figured that if the six attacked us, then we just had to defend ourselves somehow. But we didn't believe that they'd stop us, because there were few of them and we all had our own reasons—sickles [laughs]. We would cut their heads off with sickles, shovels, clubs, or whatever we had. The women made our food from a common pot and whenever there was good news (we were there eight days), or when we heard of something favorable to us, some of the girls would sing and play the guitar and entertain us. We also wrote poems, and people from Santiago came to take pictures and so forth. We had lots of visitors. They came from as far as Talquino and they sang in the evenings. They sang songs that told about our situation here. We didn't think that the *carabineros* would attack us, because there weren't many of them and we were in the right.

There aren't many good *patrones*. One in one hundred, maybe. And there are thousands like Marín. The land should be taken from all the bad ones. If the *carabineros* had wanted to fight here, we would have fought them. If they had come to open the gates we locked or to take the chains and the flag, we wouldn't have stood for it. We put up the flag because one can't fire on the flag [laughs]. There were two flags—one on each side, crossed.

I was confident that everything was going to work out because the government had said they would help the *campesinos*. Of course there were people—mainly the *empleados* who were well-off—who were against taking the *fundo*. Some *inquilinos* were against it, too, and they didn't attend the meetings and when we went to Melipilla for marches and demonstrations they didn't go, either. They are still here on the *fundo*. They didn't think we should attack the *patrón* and they didn't believe that we could do anything against him. They would ask how we thought we could win, and they thought that the *patrón* was a judge or a second God. And how many times did we have to fight him in Melipilla? We were the majority, but he won every time. In Melipilla whatever the *patrón* said was done. And if there was something that might go against him, it just stayed like it was.

We started by asking for a raise, and we kept on demanding it until he gave it to us. We had the support of all the congressmen from Melipilla, too. But then afterward he didn't fulfill his part, so we started to intimidate him, and pretty soon he came out here and had some talks with us, and he made a big joke out of it. He made a joke out of it when we showed him a biscuit that he gave us—it was really bad, filthy. "This is the kind of biscuit you give us, *patrón*," we said, and we gave it to him. He took it and started to eat it, then he said, "If a fly fell into your plate of stew you'd rather throw out the stew than eat the fly." But he was just getting started. A friend had on a wicker hat—something like the hats made of pita [maguey fiber] that they make here. The boss went up to him and took the hat and put it on his own head and said, "Look what a little hat I have to wear." That was how he made a joke out of it when we presented our complaints about the work.

One Sunday he called us all together and we waited for him but he didn't ever come. That happened twice. The second time that he was supposed to come we talked to him by telephone and told him that everyone was here and that there would be police and congressmen waiting for him, too. But he said that he wanted to work things out alone with us—with just the *campesinos*. In Melipilla, at the *inspección*, he didn't want to make any deals, so he stayed away. We left mad because he didn't want to make any arrangement with us, and we all talked it over among ourselves.

We were our own leaders. The men from the union called us and told us what we could do. The people were maddest when he took away the cuarto of land and charged ten thousand pesos per month for the pasture. He took the bread, too, and took seven thousand from some others. So the people that had the most animals ended up owing him money. That made the people here indignant. That was the first time that we struck, and everything began there.

Afterward we had to call the leaders: when the judge summoned him and the leaders from here and wanted to detain us. Then the judge tried to tell the members of the Directorate that the *patrón* couldn't come because he was sick. When they returned the next time, the *patrón* was there but the judge wasn't. That happened three times and not one of them showed up in ten months.

We finally got support from those who came out from Melipilla to offer their services. The first time, during the strike, they went to talk with a leader from Melipilla to see if we could make some deal. After that, congressmen started to give their support, but the people were still angry with the *patrón*.

I like to work the land, but I like to work it as an owner. I was getting fed up with being an *inquilino*. Also, the cuarto of land that they gave us here on the *fundo* was the worst land and it wasn't enough for us to live on. I don't know if it would be better in the city, but for me a little piece of land is best. I want my sons to get the part of the land that is theirs so that they can work it, because this land is going to be theirs. Pretty soon we are going to be old, we are going to die, so that they can have their future and their land, because they are seven brothers.

I didn't vote in the elections, because I wasn't registered. I'm going to register soon. The people here voted for Frei. Everyone.

We were thinking about moving to town before, because the way things were we didn't have enough to support ourselves.

I go to work every day, and I usually go to the theater on the *fundo* San Manuel on holidays. They have a small theater there. I go to Melipilla only when I have to do some shopping. We also buy from a truck that comes out every month.

H. Standard Interview Employed

I. Relations outside the *Fundo* System
   a)   Place where purchases are made.
   b)   Access to mass media (radio, press).
   c)   Recruitment of workers. Where is hiring done?
   d)   Presence of migrant laborers (*afuerinos*). How many?
   e)   Stability of tenure on the *fundo*.
   f)   Contacts with other *fundos*. How are they made?
   g)   Frequency of visits to town.
   h)   Frequency of outside visitors to the *fundo*: salesmen; political, union, or religious leaders.
   i)   Place where *fundo* produce is marketed.
   j)   Means of marketing *fundo* produce.
   k)   Private agricultural production for sale. Place where marketed.
   l)   Mechanization: number of machines and persons who run them.
   m)   Number of other *fundos* where previously employed. Location of *fundos*. Duration of employment.

II. Interactions within the *Fundo* System
   a)   Membership in sports clubs. Responsibilities.
   b)   Membership in labor organizations. Responsibilities.
   c)   Membership in political organizations. Responsibilities.
   d)   Principle day-to-day responsibilities on the *fundo* (outside of activities related to above-mentioned organizations):
      —at work
      —at home
      —in relation to fellow workers
      —in relation to *fundo* owners
   e)   Other responsibilities that, directly or indirectly, are imposed with some regularity.

f) Personal initiative taken to organize or support organizational activity on the *fundo*.

g) Brief history of jobs (functions) accumulated during the past two years.

h) Personal relationships on the *fundo*. Frequency of contact with others on the *fundo*. Nature of contacts.

i) Personal relationships with persons from outside the *fundo*.

j) Self-perception as to relations maintained in other places, *fundos* or towns. Do you think of yourself as isolated or as a person with outside contacts? Location and intensity of contacts.

III. Division of Labor and Social Relations

Capital farm equipment and supplies:

a) How were capital farm goods acquired?

b) Why were such goods not possessed before?

c) Why were others (*mayordomos* and *empleados*) able to acquire such goods?

Internal relations:

a) Relations between *inquilinos* and sharecroppers (*medieros*); between *inquilinos* and migrants.

b) Division of labor: how were jobs distributed? On a day-to-day basis or according to specialization?

c) Solidarity. Do the people help one another or is work performed on an each-man-for-himself basis?

d) Are some jobs performed by collaboration between individuals?

e) What do the people think is the best way to work the land?

f) Do some persons have more authority or prestige than others?

IV. Consciousness

Paternalistic consciousness:

a) The presence of a *patrón*. Is he indispensable to the operation of the *fundo*? What should he be called—entrepreneur, owner, etc.?

b) Attitude toward the majority of *patrones*. Are you acquainted with some? What are they like?

c) Main defects of the *patrón*.

d) Hypothetical attitude to the *patrón* if he had lacked these defects. Would you have wanted him to remain as owner of the *fundo*?

e)   Attitude toward worker security. Is one more secure with or without the *patrón*?

f)   Are there advantages to working with a good *patrón* rather than working alone?

g)   What is expected from a good *patrón*? What are you willing to give in return?

h)   Individual and group relations with the *patrón*. Is it better to interact with the *patrón* individually or through groups?

Reform consciousness subject to paternalism:

[an authority group has been formed, but it is dominated by the patronal structure]

a)   Peasant organization. Should the peasants be organized? Why?

b)   The nature of peasant organization. Should it be politically oriented? Should it include only the inhabitants of the *fundo* or should it include other *fundos* as well?

c)   Outside help in the struggle for reforms. Should the peasants seek the aid of outside groups or do the peasants have sufficient strength of their own? If outside aid is necessary, which groups would be most important?

d)   Possibility of similar action by other peasants. Is success possible in other cases only if the same factors are present? What is your opinion of the peasants on neighboring *fundos*? What are their attitudes? Are they capable of doing the same thing you did?

e)   The limits of reform consciousness. Is it necessary to apply pressure for reforms to the extent of using force or expropriation against the owner, or is it best to respect the owner while simply organizing in order to pressure him into making concessions?

Reform consciousness:

[the patronal structure is dominated by the peasant authority group]

a)   Do you think that the peasants all showed similar aggressiveness?

b)   Do you think that the peasants are a class with interests that conflict with those of the *patrón*, and that the conflict can only be resolved by the elimination of the *patrón*?

c)   What would happen to the country if all the *patrones* were eliminated?

d)   Is this possible? How?

e)   Should the *campesinos* fight to take the lands of the owners? Is this just? How should it be done? Are you concerned about resistance by the owners? Do you fear armed resistance? If not, what should the peasants do?

f) How should the peasants react to owner resistance?

g) Do you believe that a truly popular struggle has begun in the countryside? What consequences may it bring?

h) Does the peasantry need allies in its struggle? Which allies are the nearest? Are they those whose living conditions are most similar to yours?

General Descriptive Interview

[to be applied to leaders]

a) Causes of the movement. How long was it in the making?

b) Content of the petitions filed, and changes in content.

c) Relations among the *campesinos*. Degree of determination. Internal divisions. Attitudes toward the *patrón*.

d) External influences: leaders, government propaganda, etc.

e) Internal conditions: state of ferment, leaders.

f) Factors causing internal conditions.

g) Politization of the peasants.

h) Existence of distinct groups on the *fundo* before and after the takeover.

i) Expectations of the peasants before and after the takeover.

j) Chronological description of the process:

1) Decision to seize the land. Who took the land? How long did it take? What was the people's attitude?

2) The takeover itself: was it associated with any festivities? Were the people conscious of the importance of their act?

3) Support. Did the people feel secure or insecure? Did they rely mainly on themselves or on outside leaders, such as deputies, etc.?

4) Present conditions: degree of satisfaction, disorientation, increased politization.

5) How was a defensive strategy decided upon? Who prompted the decision?

k) Peasant attitude toward political parties. Reasons for favorable or unfavorable attitudes.

l) Detailed chronological description of events. Leaders and decision-makers.

INDEX

afuerinos: absent from Culiprán, 66
agrarian reform: attitude of politicians toward, 8-9; skepticism about, among peasants, 71-72; distortion of, 86-87; and modernization, 100-102; stages in, 103
agriculture: ascendancy of corporations in, 18 and n.; and industrial organization, 47
Aguirre Cerda, Pedro: supported by peasants, 15; elected, 21, 67, 107; peasants organize during presidency of, 110-111; campaigning for, 138; mentioned, 9
Alessandri, Arturo: in 1932 election, 8; in 1958 election, 9; and massacre of Iquique, 113
Alessandri, Jorge: supported by *empleados*, 29, 123, 125
Alessandri Palma, Arturo: elected, 21, 107
Alfonso, Pedro Enrique: in 1952 election, 9
Allende, Salvador: votes attracted by, 9; popularity of, increases, 10; receives majority of 1964 Culiprán vote, 125; peasant support for, 139
Altamirano (senator): and Culiprán takeover, 117, 141, 142; aids peasant insurrection, 127
Alwyn, A.: peasants' displeasure with, 127; and Culiprán takeover, 142
amarillos: contempt for, 31

authority: erosion of, 21-22, 24-25, 79-80; stages in erosion of, 35-40

Bossay, Luis: in 1958 election, 9

campesinos. **See** peasants
Castro, Fidel: admired by peasant leader, 109-110
Catán (landowner): as bad *patrón*, 69, 114
Caupolicán Peña (candidate for deputy): stirs up peasants, 139; alienates peasant votes, 140
Chilean Workers Federation. **See** Federación Obrera de Chile
Chonchol, Jacques: encourages peasant organization, 41
Christian Democrats (PDC): replace Ibañista movement, 9; as affected by women voters, 13; campaign among peasants, 16; as legitimizers of protest, 18; aid peasants, 32, 136; and peasant support, 33; weakening of, 36; as channel for peasant demands, 41-42; disapprove of *fundo* takeover, 110; and Culiprán takeover, 118, 142; *empleados'* affiliation with, 122, 123; peasants' displeasure with, 127; supported by peasants, 139; and peasant demands, 140, 141
civic responsibility: and civil disobedience, 4
class dynamics: within peasantry, 76-78
collective bargaining: limitations of, 22